Iron Artifacts

History, Metallurgy, Corrosion and Conservation

Iron Artifacts
History, Metallurgy, Corrosion and Conservation

SHYAM NARAIN
KAMAL K. JAIN

AGAM KALA PRAKASHAN
DELHI-110052

First Published : 2009

E-mail : shyam_narain2003@yahoo.co.in
ISBN :978- 81-7320-082-3

Published by :
Dr. Agam Prasad, M.A., Ph.D., Diploma in Museology
for **Agam Kala Prakashan**
34, Central Market, Ashok Vihar, Delhi-110052
Ph. : 27212195, 47098550, 65688806-7
Fax : 91-11-27212195
E-mail : agambooks@gmail.com, agambook@yahoo.com

Laser Typesetting by :
Elegant Printographics
319, IIIrd Floor, R.G. Complex-I,
Sector-14, Rohini, Delhi-85.
Ph. : 9891247305, 20514000

Printed at :
Salasar Imaging System
Delhi - 110035

Printed in India

PREFACE

This book is deals extensively a very important subject "Iron artifacts: History, Metallurgy, Corrosion and Conservation". It has been written mainly for metal conservators, engineers, metal conservation scientists, sculptors and students striving to acquire some background and perspective on this subject. Particularly emphasis have been given on describing the history of iron on global perspective, raw materials including nature of ferrous materials and manufacturing process of iron, deterioration and corrosion and conservation of iron artifacts. The conservation of the iron is one of the major challenges of our time and has became a share responsibilities nationally as well as internationally. With the advancement of science and technology several new materials and methods have been developed to safeguard iron and its iron antiquities. Consequently a number of books dealing with conservation of specific type of materials have come out time to time. However, a random survey indicates that there is hardly a book which covers from history of iron to philosophy and conservation of iron including techniques of casting, deterioration and metallographic studies for measurement of types and level of decay of metals.

This book is expected to useful not only for the University students, technologist, and practicising conservators of metal sculptures, artists and metallurgist but also for all those who are entrusted with the responsibilities for conserving the iron andiron artifacts. Therefore, it is proposed to produce a book which will cover the various topics in their entirety and serve as an indispensable tool for one and all.

In reading this book, it should be borne in mind that how developed iron technology on global perspective after bronze age, metallurgical identities, microstructure of metal at different temperature and various inclusions. It also explains the metallurgical factors affect the corrosion resistance, types and factors of corrosion. The last section gives the conservation methods both curative and preventive.

This book is a product of our experiences in conservation of artifacts and organizing of conservation courses and research experience in this field.

I desire to thank all those who have valuable help by supplying information. I would like to express my gratitude Dr. A.K. Mishra and Dr. K.L Garge who encouraged and help me in the preparation of this book and providing key information . My special thanks my daughters Er. Richa Punjika , Varteeka Punja, Srishti Punja and my wife Mrs. Urmila Narain for preparation of graphical data.

I would like to express my gratitude to my colleagues and friends for encouraging and proving their valuable ideas for completing this book specially to Prof. M.V. Nair; Mr. Hari Narain, Metallurgist; Mr. V.C. Sharma; Mr. Ashish Patil; Mr. Ram Pravesh Savita; Mr. Anil Risal Singh and Mr. Devendra Kumar.

Dated – October 15, 2008 **SHYAM NARAIN**
Lucknow

PUBLISHER'S NOTE

Dear reader the book entitled 'Iron Artifacts: History, Metallurgy, Corrosion and Conservation' should be kept together. If a desire to get some information about development of iron history, metallurgical, some branch of corrosion and conservation you may consult table of content and select the appropriate chapter. This will give up to date picture on subject to the readers, not merely empirical but based on scientific principles.

Dr. Agam Prasad

CONTENTS

INTRODUCTION

"Iron has changed life away from agriculture towards industry due to plentiful tools and weapons."

Iron is the best known metal that has given us weapons and tools and whose ability to suit itself to every application by way of alloying and heat treatment makes it the primary metal of technology. Iron is the most frequently encountered metal in our daily life in the form of manufactured artifacts and usually covered with a protective coating. Iron is an excellent and versatile material for construction - strong, tough, easily formed and worked, and most significantly, cheap compared to the other alternatives. The shortcomings of iron are its weight, and its propensity to rust. The three metals - iron, cobalt and nickel are called the "iron family" and are very similar. A property of the iron family for which there is no substitute at an equivalent cost is that they can be induced to provide a strong magnetic field with only small excitation by an electric current. It is a very remarkable property, therefore, an effort will be made to explain how it is formed and used.

The word iron is cognate to the German *Eisen*, which in various forms is found in all the northern European languages, though not elsewhere. In Gothic, it was E*isarn*, and in old High German, I*san*. In Greek, iron is S*íderos* and steel is C*halybicón*, stems that are encountered frequently in talking of iron, as in "siderurgy" and "chalybeate spring." "Sidereal time" is not iron time, however, but the "sider" comes from the similar Latin sidera, "stars." In Indian continent it was known as *Syam Ayas* as mentioned in Vedas, an ancient Indian literature. Iron was considered very valuable when it followed the bronze-age. It is believed that Greeks were the inventors of iron and used it for jewellery and prizes. It was used as money for times and places. The Latin for iron is *Ferrum*, from which the word in most European languages has been derived, and which appears more commonly than any other stern in words dealing with iron, especially in chemical nomenclature.

The start of iron age in India is debatable. Many travelers and investigators in the past have expressed that even as early as 1000 BC, the iron making technology was probably known to the Indians. The history advocate that metal appeared millennia ago for the use of human race because they have an interesting and pretty stone piqued someone's artistic sensibilities. Yet up to fairly recently in history, man knew nothing more about metals. They did grind up certain obviously colourful minerals, such as, emerald green malachite and rusty red hematite to use occasionally as pigments to decorate his face and his body or to paint images on the walls of caves in which they lived.

Iron artifacts are mainly excavated from sea sites and land archaeological sites. In the case of sea, these artifacts mainly come form shipwrecks that date in most of the cases after 15th Century A.D., except those of Vikings and Greeks found in Europe but still they differ from modern iron in their composition and manufacturing techniques.

Archeological iron materials have some of the most difficult problems confronted by the conservator. The techniques of preserving this material has been carefully studied and a variety of techniques developed. The following sections describe the most applicable and useful approaches and conservation techniques that can be utilized to process and document the archeological materials. For the successful treatment of any artifact requires that the conservator be familiar with the deterioration and corrosion processes, as well as the physical and chemical properties of the iron . The text containing history of iron on the global perspective, nature of materials and manufacturing process of iron, casting and molding, corrosion, steps of conservation including documentation, cleaning and storage.

From the moment of manufacture the iron and its alloys, react with their environment and begin a corrosion process that converts them to more stable compounds.

It is essential that the conservator be aware of the corrosion products that result from exposure to different environments before applied of a suitable and competent conservation techniques. The nature of the corrosion products determines the technique and procedures that can be effectively used. Consequently, corrosion is briefly covered. The corrosion of iron can be discussed in terms of iron artifacts in terrestrial environments with temperate, tropical, and desert subdivisions as well as aquatic environments with salt and fresh water . A more simplified approach and more to point is to look at the corrosion resulting from the interacting effects of wet, dry, aerobic, and anaerobic environments i.e. the presence of oxygen and moisture. In sea water various variables, along with temperature, pH and the presence of aggressive anions such as chloride in the water, determine the rates and types of corrosion.

Salt water corrosion on the iron artifact is stressed here, with emphasis on excavated archeological burial iron artifacts . For clarity, however, other environmental conditions are briefly considered. The corrosion of iron is included on the wide and global perspective . The archaeological excavation and findings had witnessed in various parts of the world, bringing to the surface a large number of artifacts of numerous kinds. In excavation of some archaeological sites , due to lack of, proper planning, under standing of deterioration of materials and non-availability of conservation facilities, much of the materials excavated has been lost for ever. This is very unfortunate, as these invaluable iron artifacts would have definitely survived for a longer time if left alone on the seabed or under excavated sites in the mother's hands where they were resting.

Marine environment extends from sea where seawater is indirect contact with contaminants and an artifact outside the sea, where winds and air currents carry out the sea salt as contaminants. The environment above seawater, shores, coastal areas, are marine atmosphere. In marine archaeological artifacts are mostly get from shipwrecks. So the under-water environment will dealt with marine atmosphere is the environment and above the seawater, shores, coastal regions and of islets in the oceans. It is a region with high humidity, which can be up to 100% relative humidity. For example near the seashores, the surfaction is very high. Sodium chloride and other salt particles are present in high quantities in the atmosphere.

The salts get into the atmosphere due to surf actions and transportation by air currents. In some regions the air may be super-saturated with sodium chloride and resultant corrosion is very fast in such areas, but as the distance from the sea increases the amount of sodium chloride in the air decreases, so that the rate of corrosion decreases.

The underwater environment is formed by the sea, which covers 71% of the Earth's surface. It is characterized by the presence of a solid - liquid interface .On the based on this characteristic, the under-water environment at wreck sites can be divided into:

- Environment where artifact- seawater- interface is present;
- Environment where artifact-seawater-atmosphere interface occurs.;
- Environment where artifact- sediment- interstitial water of sediment interface is observed;
- Environment where artifact - sediment - interstitial water interface .

Such interface boundaries are sites for a wide variety of chemical, physical and biological reactions. The main factors affecting these reactions, i.e. corrosion in case of metals in the underwater environment are ; a: The seawater, b: the sediments, and c: the marine biota.

Water is a unique solution, which is composed of complex mixtures of chemical constituents, particulate matter and gas bubbles. Water is a universal solvent and acts as a solvent in seawater, bringing about ionization of salts and acting as a transport medium for hydrated ions i.e. electrolytes. chloride ions, sodium ions, sulphate ions, magnesium ions, calcium ions, potassium ions, carbonates and bi-carbonates make up 99.5% of the chemical constituents of seawater, while the minor chemical species in it are iron, silicon, borate and phosphate. (Florian M.L.E , 1988: 1- 20). Salinity is the amount of sodium ions and chloride ions present in water.

Oxygen and carbon dioxide are the major gases present in dissolved state in water. Oxygen originates from the atmosphere, biological activity photosynthesis and degradation of organic matter. The amount of oxygen in water varies from 0 to 8.5ml / liter. The availability of dissolved oxygen affects the rate and type of corrosion. Carbon dioxide gives carbonate and bicarbonate ions , forming a carbon dioxide-carbonate equilibrium, which controls the alkalinity or pH of water. It acts as a buffer system to maintain the pH of water between 7.5 to 8.5 and also controls the deposition of sediments on the iron artifacts.

Organic and inorganic materials are continuously being added to the water, some in dissolved form while the remaining as suspended particles. These dissolved matters, due to chemical precipitation, adsorption and biological processes are changed into solids, which settle down as part of sediments. As the suspended particles, they also slowly settle down on the floor. Plankton in region of high activity forms part of the marine sediment after death.

The physical properties of sediments depend upon the particle size, degree of interstitial compactness and the interstitial water content of sediments. The amount of interstitial water diminishes with increase in sediment depth. Interstitial water differs from seawater in having a higher salinity, greater amount of carbon dioxide, hydrogen sulphide, ammonia, iron, magnese, silicon oxides are dissolved than seawater, but lower amounts of the oxides of sulpher and magnesium. The rate of deterioration in burial artifacts to be higher than when only submerged in seawater. Metals show accelerated corrosion because of less amount of oxygen and presence of reducing bacteria in anaerobic conditions.

The biological organisms, which affect the deterioration of iron artifacts in water, are mainly the fouling assemblages and marine bacteria. Their distribution in sea is governed by such environmental factors as water, salinity, temperature, depth, pressure, nutrient and different sediment properties. Some of the important organisms of the fouling communities which are most commonly associated with marine iron artifacts are corals, coralline algae, shellfish, tube worms, etc.

It is not clearly understood why the surface concretions formed by these organisms, in some cases act as protective shield while in other cases accelerate corrosion in those regions. All fouling organisms, being dependent on oxygen for growth, are normally absent in anoxic environments and in sediments.

The sulphate-reducing bacteria has a primary importance in case of deterioration of iron artifacts. They are responsible for corrosion of iron in anaerobic conditions. They may also be found in the marine concretion layer in the marine environment and calcareous and siliceous deposition in the ground on the iron artifacts and continue corrosion carries on .

In the marine and under ground, surface environment a number of corrosion products are form due corrosion factors and try to go in mother state. In some environment the iron artifact get an equilibrium state and retain their identities. Chlorides are the main culprit for deterioration of iron artifacts, it forms a complex corrosion products. Oxygen , carbonate , sulphate are equally responsible for corrosion and forms the corrosion products as oxides, carbonates, sulphate , hydroxides of the iron artifacts.

Humidity and the presence of corrosion stimulators will normally cause corrosion to develop red , black or brown oxide into a thicker crust of minerals. The main mass is composed of iron oxides and carbonates . This mass containing ferric Oxyhydroxides (FeO.OH), the bulk being in the form of red/brown/yellow, Goethite (αFeO.OH) with some orange , Lepidocrocite (γFeO.OH), there can also be amorphous Limonite (FeO.OH), Siderite ($FeCO_3$) and Calcium carbonate . In the humid condition and oxygen free deposits often appear black because of iron II sulphide formed by sulphate reducing bacteria. The layer can be hard and shiny or sludge like with much of the metal.

Below the outer rust coloured oxides, the black oxide magnetite (Fe_3O_4) which forms in region of low oxygen. Where corrosion is complete, the metal is replaced entirely by black dense lustrous magnetite underlying a greater or lesser zone of brown oxides. The original surface can be detected by careful investigative cleaning; the original surface can be seen as a denser zone of corrosion which unlike the overlying bulk, does not incorporate grains of sand etc.

In certain moist oxygenated deposits, which occur in the both cases sea and soiled , it is found that all the oxidized iron of an artifact has migrated into the surrounding environment and small wrought iron artifacts may disperse completely for a years. Cast iron artifacts from the sea always remains solid, even totally corroded and encased within a crust of ferrous concretion. Under this crust the surface of the corroded artifact is to be very soft and often consists of a matrix of rusty corrosion products with small lustrous inclusions. These are flakes of graphite of grey cast iron which survive, having been the cathodic part of an iron/carbon galvanic corrosion cell, while the base iron corrodes preferentially. the iron oxide and carbonates formed are held in situ between the graphite flakes and so on the shape of the artifact, in a mineralized state, is preserved.

On some occasions it is found that heavily corroded iron artifacts are stable after excavation, but it is more usual to find that after some weeks or years, lumps or as cleaned iron corrosion product pseudomorphs begins to disintegrate. The artifacts splits up in the case of wrought iron along the direction of working, to reveal damp, dark orange brown spots. It has been noted that artifacts which still retain metallic iron even though this is only vestigial, are those which are most likely to break up, the totally corroded or hollow artifacts often appear stable.

The surface of concretion is occasionally covered by a thin white or pale brown crust, but more often it is coated with a loose deposit of rusty corrosion products .These outer layers contain a high proportion of calcium and magnesium carbonate and hydroxide and also Siderite ($Fe CO_3$) ,but inside they consist almost entirely of the oxides and hydrated oxides of iron. Silica (SiO_2) and black iron sulphide (Fe S) may also occur. Concretions found within marine sediment, where oxygen is relatively scarce, contain higher proportions of Lepidocrocite ($\gamma FeO.OH$), Black Magnetite (Fe_3O_4), Magnetic Sulphide, Pyrorrhotite and other compounds which are unstable in atmospheric conditions and difficult to identify may also be present.

Conditions from which true metal might be retrieved, since iron is so base this will occur only in the presence of phosphate layer or where oxygen is absent. Iron may be preserved either by passivation in deposits of high redox potential and pH due to stiffing by oxide/carbonate crusts or by immunity in deposits of low redox potential, that is where oxygen is low. Preservation can be prevented by the activity of sulphate reducing bacteria, the presence of chloride ions, or enhanced by phosphates in deposits of low redox potential.

If the chemical and electrolytic techniques are not applicable and so manual mechanical methods using small tools or, more commonly, air abrasion with continuous visual examination alone can be used to cleaning extremely intensive. Ironwork with only a thin layer of corrosion products overlying metal is rare in archaeological artifact but common in historic and ethnographic materials. It would be possible to strip such artifacts by dissolving the iron oxides. This could be achieved with acids but since iron is a base metal, it too will dissolve in many acids and so become etched. Commercial rust removers are usually based on mild inhibited organic acids or phosphoric acids, but they often leave a layer of visible protective deposit over the metal.

In electrolytic cleaning, iron is cathodically protected by electric current from etching. However, all these methods ruthlessly expose existing pits in the metal surface, which is unsightly, and cause plating and inlays to react or become displaced. Today, because of these dangers, archaeological iron even of this type is never stripped. Abrasive mechanical methods are preferred.

Until shown by radiography or strong pull on a magnet to be otherwise , that small wrought iron artifacts covering concretions then cleaning is to be taken in another way not like cast iron .

Where concretion is solid then removed from the artifact before storage otherwise stabilization is difficult to achieve. The soft corroded surface of the artifact may contain much important information about artifact's history which would only be obtained if such iron artifact were cleaned. Selective cleaning may thus seem to be necessary, although such action would bring about the ultimate destruction of the cleaned artifacts.

The visual examination of the corrosion crust is important to identify any organic pseudomorph as well as inorganic deposition. It should be in the normal practice the using precautionary measures, suitable and competent conservation methods and techniques for cleaning the artifacts on the sites and in the conservation laboratory.

The Chemical and electrolytic techniques for cleaning is not applicable at excavated sites. So manual and mechanical methods using small tools with continuously visual examination are advisable. The recommended methods and techniques should be used for cleaning in the laboratory after proper investigation and documentation. The protective coating/s can be applied with suitable coating materials.

CHAPTER-ONE

HISTORY
(History of Iron on Global Perspective)

Introduction

Historians believe that the Egyptians were the first people to work with small amounts of iron around thousand years ago. The metal used by them was apparently extracted from meteorites. Evidence of what is believed to be the first example of iron mining and smelting points to the ancient culture is now in Turkey. Because iron was a first superior material for the manufacture of weapons and tools than any other known metal, its production was a closely guarded secrets. However, the basic technique was simple, and the use of iron gradually spread. It was useful in compare to other materials but it had disadvantages also. The quality of the tools was highly variable which made from iron. It was depending on the region from which the iron ore was taken and the method used to extract the iron. The importance of the chemical nature of the carbon to the metal's hardness during the extraction were not understood ancient time. The Practices varied widely in different parts of the world. There is evidence that the Chinese were able to melt and cast iron implements in very early, the Japanese produced amazing results with steel in small amounts, as evidenced by heirloom swords dating back centuries. Similar break through were made in the middle east and India, but the processes never emerged into the rest of the world. The Europeans had lacked of the methods for heating iron to the melting point. They slowly burned iron ore with wood in a clay-lined oven to produce iron. The iron never quite melted but separated from the surrounding rock. Instead, it formed a crusty slag which was removed by hammering. The repeated heating and hammering process mixed oxygen with the iron oxide to produce iron, and removed the carbon from the metal. The result of heating and hammering was nearly pure iron which easily shaped with hammers and tongs . It was kept a good edges due to its softness . Because the metal was shaped or wrought by hammering so called wrought iron.

Tools and weapons brought to Europe from the East. Where they were made up of iron that had been melted and cast into shape. When iron retaining more carbon, cast iron ,is harder than wrought iron and will hold a cutting edge. However, it is also more brittle than wrought iron. The European knew that Easterners had better iron, but not the processes involved in fashioning stronger iron products. To discover the process entire nations launched their efforts.

The first known European breakthrough in the production of cast iron, which led quickly to the first practical steel, did not come until 1740. Benjamin Huntsman took out a patent for the melting of materials for the production of steel springs to be used in clock making in that year. The procedure was widely adopted. To melt wrought iron, Huntsman used a blast furnace in a clay crucible and added carefully measured amounts of pure charcoal to the melted metal. Resulting strong and flexible alloy was formed and used to cast into springs. Huntsman was originally interested only in making better clocks. His crucible steel led directly to the development of nautical chronometers in turn to made global navigation possible by allowing mariners to precisely determine their direction and position. Infact , he had also shared in invention of modern metallurgy.

Archaeologists and historians believed that iron came in existence around 1500 BC. It was next great development in metallurgy involves a metal which is the most abundant in the earth's crust. Iron have too high melting point for primitive furnaces to extract it in pure form from its ore. The best qualities that can be achieved is a cluster of globules of iron mixed with sludgy impurities. By repeated heating and hammering this unpromising substance can be turned into a useful metal, until the impurities are literally forced out. A few iron artifacts dating from before 1600 BC have been found.

1. The magic form of iron

It is believed that the Hittites were the first people to work on iron, in Anatolia in around 1500 BC. An archaeological evidences shows that people of India work on iron from about 1700 BC. Iron is simple in form and less hard than bronze .Therefore used as weapons were very nominal, but it seems to have had an immediate appeal - perhaps as the latest achievement of technology in iron. The mysterious qualities of iron was being changeable, through heating and hammering which from a certain intrinsic magic and showed a magic form .It was the metal in meteorites which fallen from the sky. It had much value which was attached to iron , a famous letter of about 1250 BC, written by a Hittite king to accompany an iron dagger-blade which he was sending to a monarch fellow.

2. The discovery of steel : A global perspective

During the 11th century BC , it has been discovered that iron can much be improve in their qualities. It was reheated in a furnace with charcoal which containing carbon, some of the carbon was transferred to the iron. During this process iron became harden and the effect was considerably superior qualities than previous. The hot metal was rapidly reduced in temperature by cold water. This process was known as quenching. Now the new material was steel. It can be worked (or 'wrought') just like softer iron, and it will keep a finer edge, capable of being honed to sharpness. Gradually, from the 11th century onwards, steel replaces bronze weapons in the Middle East, birth place of the Iron Age.

3. Advent of Cast iron

There is a story that iron has been heated and hammered, but never melted. The melting point of iron is 1528°C which is too high in respect to primitive furnaces. The primitive furnace can reach about 1300°C and were adequate for melt to copper. The melting point of copper is 1083°C. It was the limitation of the primitive furnace. This limitation is overcome when around 513 BC when the Chinese traditionally developed a furnace hot enough to melt iron, enabling them to produce the world's first cast iron. In this they are a thousand and more years ahead of the western world. It is believed that the first iron foundry was made in England in AD 1161. By that time the Chinese have already pioneered the structural use of cast iron, using it sometimes for the pillars of full-size pagodas.

By the middle bronze age, increasing numbers of smelted iron artifacts distinguishable from meteoric iron were appeared throughout the Levant, the Mediterranean, Antolia, Egypt, Mesopotamia and Indian sub continent. At some places, their use for ceremonial purposes. At that time iron was more expensive than gold and known as an expensive metal. The sources suggested that iron was being created in some places then as a by-product of copper refining, as sponge iron, and was not reproducible by the metallurgy of that time.

Iron was systematically produced from a large source of meteoritic iron in Anatolia. The earliest systematic production and use of iron implements originated there. Iron was widely used around 1200 BC in the Middle East .On the same time Sub-Saharan production of iron began , and seems to have been clearly an independent invention. Places that contained iron developed a prominence in the last millennium BC that would last into the future. Military technology designed to complement the use of iron came from Assyria. At Troy a mace head found in 1902 of the dated to around 1200 BC. It is likely to Assyrian manufacture. Assyria, in fact, may have considered Troy an outpost of itself. The iron trade between the two places was well established at that time. The Assyrians secrets the production and guarding of iron trade.

4. Ancient Iron Age Near East

It is believed that the Iron Age in the ancient near east to have begun with the discovery of iron in the late 2nd millennium BC around (circa 1300 BC)with smelting and smithing techniques in Antolia . This technique was spread rapidly as iron weapons and replaced bronze weapons by the early 1st millennium BC.The use of iron weapons by the Hittites was a major factor in the rapid rise and spread of the Hittite Empire. The iron technology developed and propagated equally into both Asia and Europe with Hittite expansion. The sea-peoples and the related philistines are often associated with the introduction of iron technology into Asia, as are the Dorians with respect to Greece. The Assyrian Empire had trade contacts with the area in which iron technology was first developed at the time that it was developing.

5. Iron in Europe

The Iron working was introduced in Europe around 1000 BC. Probably it came from Asia. Iron working was slowly spread northwards and westwards.

a. Eastern Europe

The Iron age came in early 1st millennium BC in the Eastern Europe . The Iron age begins with the Koban and the Chernogorovka and Novocerkask cultures from c.900 BC in the Pontic steppe and the Caucasus. It was spreading to Hallstatt C via the alleged "Thraco-Cimmerian" migrations around 800 BC. The Iron age spreads in the west with the Celtic expansion from the 6th century BC by the Hallstatt culture. The Iron Age with technology reaches in Poland by late Lusation culture in about the 6th century and followed in some areas by the Pomerian culture.

The ethnic ascriptions of many Iron age cultures has been bitterly contested, as the roots of Germany and Slaves were sought in this area.

b. Central Europe

The Iron Age in Central Europe is generally divided in the early and late iron age. The early Iron Age was Hallstatt culture and known as HaC . Its period was 800-450 BC, and the late Iron Age was La Tene culture was beginning in 450 BC. In the Central Europe Iron age ends with the Roman Conquest.

c. Italy

The Villanovans culture was probably introduced the Iron age in Italy. This culture was also considered as Bronze age culture, Etruscan civilization is regarded as part of Iron age. The Etruscan Iron age was then ended with the rise and conquest of the Romans , which conquered the last Etruscan city of Velzna in 265 BC.

d. British Isles

The Iron Age lasted from about the 5th century AD in the British Isles until the Roman conquest and until the 5th century AD in non-Romanised parts. Defensive structures dating from this time are often impressive, for example the broche of northern Scotland and the hill forts that dotted the rest of the islands.

e. Northern Europe

The Iron Age is divided into the pre- Roman Iron age and the Roman Iron age in northern Europe. This is known as the migrated period. Northern Germany and Denmark was dominated by the Jastorf culture, whereas the culture of the southern half of the Scandinavia was dominated by the very similar Gregan Iron age. Scandinavia including Finland and Northern Balticum shows a small-scaled iron producing country in very early, but a further dating is currently impossible. The time varies from 3000 BC-1000 AD. Metalworking and Asbestos- Ceramic pottery are somewhat synonymous in Scandinavia due to the latter's capability to resist and preserve heat. The iron ore used is believed to have been iron sand such as red soil, because its high phosphorus content can be identified in slag. Together with asbestos ware axes belonging to the Ananjino Culture are sometimes found. The Asbestos-Ceramic remains a mystery, because there are other adiabatic vessels with unknown usage.

6. Iron in South and East Asia

a. Indian Subcontinent

From the various studies it has been possible to establish to approximation of a chronological order of different culture in Indian subcontinent . It is mentioned in various literature that the last de-glaciations started around 15000 BC in the Kashmir area and the Holocene period could be placed around 11,000-10,000 BC (Jafery M.S. 1988:16-103).

The Mesolithic culture started around c. 6000 BC and Neolithic period started around c.2400 BC and settled life started with agriculture, handmade pottery and ground stone tools in this period . This culture is distinguished in three phases . In the third phase, we find the extensive use of metal around c.1400-1000BC. Iron appeared around c.2000-800 BC and with the advent of Iron the Gangatic plain has been colonized (,Jafery M .S. 1988 and Roy T.N. 1983:165-181)

The recent findings of archaeology suggest that from the Mesolithic period (Iron age) the Indian culture in India was started. During the Mesolithic period the Aryans were shifted to the Gangatic plain (Roy T.N. 1983:165-181) . This was the period of Mahabharata with the capital at Hastinapur near Delhi.A major incident which happened during this time was the Mahabharata battle. In this battle the swords, spears, axes arrows were used. In the Mahabhrata it is mentioned that a life size iron statue of Bhima was presented to Dhristrashtra and he broke it in the pieces with his arms . Alexander the Great defeated Porus of Taxila in c.326 B.C. and received a gift of steel from him(Jafery M.S. 1988:116-103). Innumerable inscriptions of Ashoka are the oldest surviying Indian written documents of any historic significance. They consist of edicts engraved on rocks and pillars scattered all over India .For making inscriptions on stone one would require the deployment of very sharp chisels and it could, therefore, be inferred that technique of producing hard tools of rock cutting was well known in that period. Ashoka built a monastery first in Bodh Gaya in the third century BC. Recent excavation of the foundation at this place have yielded metals including iron clamps, coins and precious stone.

Beginning from the early century of the Christian era, iron has found to be used extensively. In this connection the Iron pillar measuring in 7.2m length of the Mehrauli, Delhi , near the Qutub Minar is a very good example for its excellent preservation qualities . An analysis revealed that it contains 99.72% Iron, 0.08% carbon ,0.006% sulpher, and 0.11% phosphorus (Tylecote R.F. 1976 :11,25,59-63) .But the new analysis shows that the pillar contains zinc and lead also(Jafery M.S. 1988:16-103) .

An archaeological evidence ratify that most of the area was having iron mines in India from the Kashmir to Assam and different types of ores were found. In Kashmir -Magnetite, Hematite, Limonite and other sedimentary ores are found. Panjab and Uttranchal mines have Magnetite, brown Hematite ores of iron. The Chota Nagpur area of Bihar was famous for various type of Iron ores. Talchar, Sambhalpur were rich for the iron ores,. The Khasi and Jantia hills of the Assam now in Meghalaya have Titaniferous magnetic iron., Magnetite sand in Mirzapur is famous. Alwar , Ajmer, Jaipur, Jodhpur, Kota, Bharatpur, Bundi have hematite, magnetite, limonite ores . The lateritic ore of Iron in Ujjain, Mansore, Jhabua, Baster, Mandla, Rewa and Bundel khand is famous(Jafery M.S. 1988:16-103and Roy T.N. 1983:165-181).

The archeological evidences show that Manjhi in Bihar, Allahpur, Aterenjikhera, Bhardwaj Ashram (300AD-600AD), Hulaskhera (700BC-700AD), Jajmau (600BC-600AD), Kausambi (PGW-500 AD), Sringvergpura (700BC-600AD) in U.P the people used iron (Agrawal O.P.,Hari Narain,Jaiprakash 1991:12-26and Roy T.N. 1983:165-181)

The iron pillar at Dhar supposed to be the highest iron pillar of 12.5m and weight about 7000 Kg (Mahmud Syed Jafery 1988:16-103and Tylecote R.F. 1976:11,25,59-63) , is believed to be constructed in the 12th century AD as a victory pillar. Another iron pillar 3836 mm high is kept in the premises of the temple of Anchaleshwar on Mount Abu. Both the places are very near to Ujjain(Jafery M.S. 1988:16-103) . The historians have mentioned that Ujjain was a big industrial center for iron during c.500-200 BC.

Archaeological sites in India, such as Malhar, Dadupur, Raja Nala Ka Tila and Lahuradewa in the state of Utter Pradesh show iron implements in the period between c.1800 BC - 1200 BC. By the early 13th century BC, iron smelting was definitely practiced on a bigger scale in India.It is suggesting that the date the technology's inception may well be placed as early as the 16th century BC.

The another early Iron Age archaeological culture of the Indian Subcontinent have the Black and Red ware culture. This culture is dated to roughly the 12th - 9th centuries BC, and associated with the post-Rigvedic civilization. It reached from the upper Gangatic plain in Utter Pradesh to the eastern Vindhya range and West Bengal.

Perhaps, although certainly by, the high quality in south India by the crucible technique around early c.300BC. During the c.200AD steel was being produced in south India. In this system, high-purity wrought iron, charcoal, and glass were mixed in crucibles and heated until the iron melted and absorbed the carbon. The resulting high-carbon steel, called wootz steel. It was exported throughout Asia and Europe.

b. Eastern Asia

Cast-iron artifacts are found in China of the Zhou dynasty of the 6th century BC. The Iron age culture of the Tibetan Plateau has tentatively been associated with the Zhang Zhung culture . Which is described in early Tibetan writings. Near the city of Gaocheng in Shijiazhung now Hebei province, an iron-bladed bronze tomahawk dating back to the 14th century BC was excavated in the year 1972. After a scientific examination, the iron was shown to be made from aero siderite.

Iron artifacts were introduced to Korean Peninsula the through trade with chiefdoms and state-level societies in the yellow Sea area in the fourth century BC, just at the end of the Warring States period but before the Western Han Dynasty began. The iron was first introduced to chiefdoms located along North Korean river valleys that flow into the Yellow Sea such as the Cheongcheon and Taedong Rivers . Iron production quickly followed in the 2nd century BC, and iron implements came to be used by farmers by the 1st century AD in southern Korea . The earliest cast-iron axes in southern Korea is found in the Geum River basin. At approximately the same time complex chiefdoms of Proto- historic Korea developed that were the precursors of early states such as Silla,Baekje,Gogueyeo, and Gaya . In this period the iron ingots that indicated the wealth or prestige of the deceased became an important mortuary item.

7. Iron in Sub-Saharan Africa

The Nok civilization which was spread in the West Africa, became the first iron smelting people before 1000 BC. They were started iron and copper working then continued to spread southward through the continent and working reach to the Cape around 200 AD. The Bantu farming communities adopted the widespread use of revolutionized iron. They were driving out the stone tool for using hunter and gatherer societies. They were encountered as they expanded to farm wider areas of savannah. The technologically Bantu were superior. Bantu spread across southern Africa and became rich and powerful, producing iron for tools and weapons in large, industrial quantities. Sub-Saharan Africa was still in the iron age with the arrival of European explorers in the 19th century.

CHAPTER-TWO

METALLURGY
(Nature of Ferrous Materials and Manufacturing Process of Iron)

Introduction

Iron is the fourth abundant element and second most abundant in metal in the crust of the Earth . It is highly reactive and rarely occur in free state. Its symbol is Fe, atomic number 26, and atomic weight 55.847. It is a malleable, tough, silver-gray, magnetic metal. It melts at 1540°C, boils at 2800°C, and has a density of 7.86 g/cm^3. The four stable, naturally occurring isotopes have masses of 54, 56, 57, and 58. The main ores are hematite Fe_2O_3, ; limonite Fe_2O_3 $3H_2O$. Pyrite FeS_2, and chromite $Fe(CrO_2)_2$, mined as ores for sulphur and chromium respectively. The plentiful iron pyrite, FeS_2 is not an acceptable ore because sulphur is a deleterious impurity in iron, and expensive to remove in refining. The usual ferrous sulphide, FeS, can add sulphur stochiometrically to form crystalline FeS_2, known as the mineral pyrite. This is from the Greek pyrites, from pyr, "fire," and meaning something made of fire. When struck by iron, it will produce luminous sparks that can be used to ignite tinder to make fire. Pyrite is a good source of sulphur, but not a good source of iron because of the sulphur, which ruins iron and is hard to separate from it . Pyrite is also found in coal, where it adds unwelcome sulphur to the fuel. Good crystals of pyrite are an excellent brassy yellow colour, leading fools to mistake it for gold. However, it is hard and light, not soft and heavy, so it is easily distinguished from gold. In small flakes, however, it could be deceiving, and especially because it is very often associated with gold. Pyrite crystallizes in the cubic system, and its crystals are typically cubes and pyritohedrons. A pyritohedron has 12 pentagonal faces, but the pentagons are not regular, so the solid is not a dodecahedron. Crystals do not have 5-fold axes. The cube faces are usually striated each face at right angles to the neighboring faces. Hardness, 6.0 to 6.5, and density 4.8 to 5.1 g/cc. When heated, sulphur is driven off and the iron oxidized to magnetite.

Hematite Fe_2O_3, magnetite Fe_3O_4, and siderite $FeCO_3$ are the chief iron ores in the form of oxides and carbonate . The oxides are ferrous oxide FeO and ferric oxide Fe_2O_3. Ferrous oxide is not stable against partial oxidation to Fe_3O_4 or $FeO.Fe_2O_3$. This hard, black substance is magnetite and important ore of iron. Iron forms the hydroxide minerals as lepidocrocite and goethite.The general formula is FeO(OH). It joins magnesium in the carbonate pyroaurite.

Depending on the condition, iron is a good reducing agents and having 2^+, 3^+, or 6^+ oxidation state. The ferrous and ferric ion is present as a distinct unit in most of iron compounds. Ferrous compounds are usually light yellow to dark green-brown in color; the hydrated ion, $Fe(H_2O)_6^{2+}$, in many compounds and solution is light green in colour. This hydrated ion of iron has little tendency to form coordination complexes except with strong reagents such as cyanide ion, polyamines, and porphyrins. The ferric ion has a strong tendency to hold anions due to its highly charge (3^+) and small size. The hydrated ion, $Fe(H_2O)_6^{3+}$, which is found in solution, combines with OH^-, F^-, Cl^-, CN^-, SCN^-, N_3^-, $C_2O_4^{2-}$, and other anions to form coordination complexes.

Proper knowledge of materials constituting artifacts is very important. Firstly to have a good understanding of the corrosion processes affecting the artifacts and secondly for choosing and selecting the right method of conservation and avoiding irreparable damage being done to the invaluable artifacts.

As we know that the iron is one of the most common elements on earth. The every construction of man contains at least a little iron. It is also one of the oldest metals and was first fashioned into useful and ornamental objects around thousand of years ago.

Pure iron is a soft, grayish-white metal and never found in free form in nature. The only pure iron known to exist naturally comes from fallen meteorites. Most of the iron is found in minerals formed by the combination of iron with other elements. The most common is oxides of the iron . Minerals near the surface of the earth that have the highest iron content are known as iron ores and are mined commercially.

Various types of iron may be obtained from the iron ores through several chemical processes. The blast furnace process is the most common process to production of pig iron .Pig iron contains about 92-94% iron and 3-5% carbon and smaller and trace amounts of other elements. Pig iron has only limited uses and most of this iron goes on to a steel mill where it is converted into various steel alloys by further reducing the carbon content and adding other elements such as manganese and nickel to give the steel specific properties.

1. Raw Materials uses for production of Iron

To the production of iron, iron ores, coke, sinter, and limestone are used as raw materials in a blast furnace. Iron ores are mainly iron oxides including magnetite, hematite, limonite, iron carbonates, Iron sulphides and many other rocks. These ores contain from 70-20% iron. Coke is a substance made by heating coal until it becomes almost pure carbon. Sinter is made of low grade, finely divided iron ore , which is roasted with coke and lime to remove a large amount of the impurities. Limestone occurs naturally and is a source of calcium carbonate. Other metals are some times mixed with iron in the production of various types of steel, such as chromium, nickel, manganese, molybdenum, and tungsten.

2. Manufacturing Process

a. The Extraction of Ores and Refining Process

Before using the iron ores in a blast furnace, it must be extracted from the ground and partially refined to remove most of the impurities. Iron ore is extracted through open pit mining in which the surface of the ground is removed by heavy machines, often over a very large area, to expose the ore beneath. In cases where it is not economical to remove the surface, shafts are dug into the earth, with side tunnels to follow the layer of ores.

After digging the ores from the pits or tunnels, the first of all the mined ore is crushed , broken in to small pieces and sorted. The best grades of ore contain over 60% iron. Lower grades are treated and refined to remove various contaminants before the ore is shipped to the blast furnace. Collectively, these refining methods are called beneficiation and include further crushing, washing with water to float sand and clay away, and magnetic separation, palletizing, and sintering. Depleted is high iron content ore, these refining techniques have become increasingly important. The refined ore is then loaded on trains or ships and transported to the blast furnace site.

The most of the ores are rich enough and do not need any further concentration. In some cases, the oxide ores may be concentrated by washing with water, which washes away the gangue particles leaving behind the heavy ore particles. This method of concentration is called gravity separation method. In the roasting and calcinations the dressed and concentrated ore is heated with a little coke and excess of air in shallow kilns. In this process following change may be observed

Iron pyrites get roasted to its oxides

$$4FeS_2 + 4O_2 \longrightarrow 2Fe_2O_3 + SO_2\uparrow$$

The impurities like phosphorus, sulphur and arsenic are removed as their volatile oxides during the roasting

$$P_4{+}5O_2 \longrightarrow P_4O_{10}\uparrow \text{ (phosphorus penta oxide)}$$
$$S + O_2 \longrightarrow SO_2\uparrow$$
$$4As + 10O_2 \longrightarrow 2As_2O_{10}\uparrow$$

The moisture is removed from the $3Fe_2O_3.3H_2O$ which is obtained by the roasting.

$$Fe_2O_3.3H_2O \longrightarrow Fe_2O_3 + 3H_2O\uparrow$$

Carbonates ores get decomposed to ferrous oxide

$$FeCO_3 \longrightarrow FeO + CO_2\uparrow$$

b. Charging the blast furnace

The charge is consisting of roasted ore and lime stone introduced into furnace by cup and cone arrangment. Lime stone is generally used as a basic flux to remove the acid impurities like silica present in iron ores. If impurities in the ore are of the basic nature such as carbonate of calcium, magnesium, silica then added as acidic flux to form slag. The function of the cook is to reduce the ore into metal and to melt iron. The ore is blended with other ore and goes to the blast furnace after processing. A blast furnace

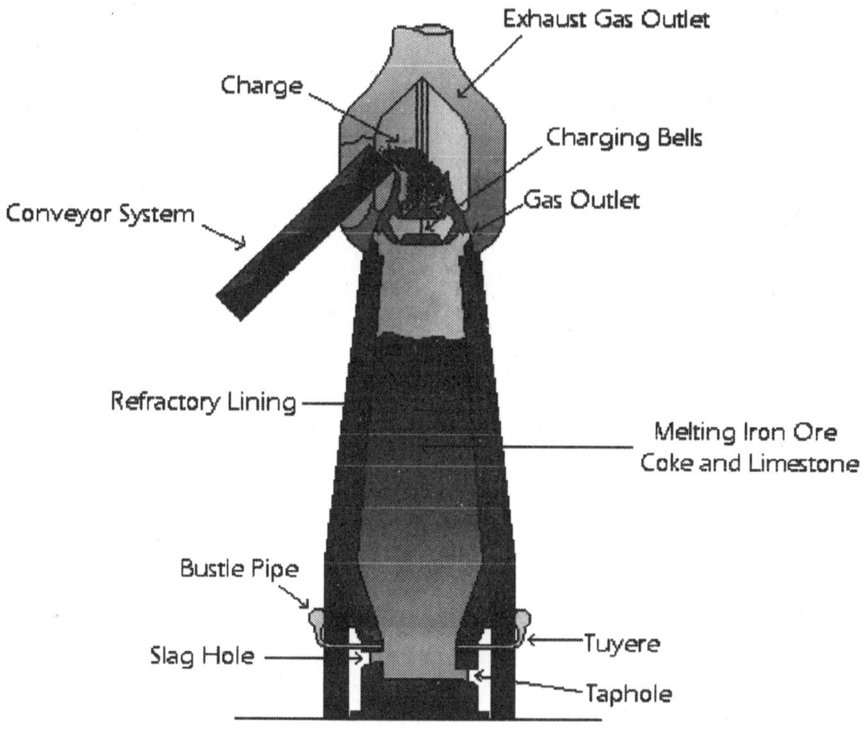

Blast Furnace

is a tower-shaped structure, made of steel, and lined with refractory or heat-resistant bricks. The mixture of raw material with charge enters at the top of the blast furnace. At the bottom of the furnace, the very hot air is blown and blasted in through nozzles called tuye'res. The coke burns in the presence of the hot air. The oxygen in the air reacts with the carbon in the coke to form carbon monoxide. The carbon monoxide then reacts with the iron ore to form carbon dioxide and pure iron.

c. Separating of the iron from slag

The melted iron sinks to the bottom of the furnace. The limestone combines with the rock and other impurities in the ore to form a slag which is lighter than the iron floats on the top of the furnace. As the volume of the charge is reduced, more is continually added at the top of the furnace. The iron and slag are drawn off separately from the bottom of the furnace. The melted iron might go to a further alloying process, or might be cast into ingots called pigs. The slag is carried away for disposal.

d. Treating the gases

The hot gases produced in the chemical reactions are drawn off at the top and routed to a gas cleaning plant where they are cleaned and scrubbed and sent back into the furnace.The remaining carbon monoxide is useful to the chemical reactions going on within the furnace. A blast furnace normally runs day and night for several years. Eventually the brick lining begins to crumble, and the furnace is then shut down for maintenance.

e. Quality Control

The blast furnace operation is highly instrumented and is monitored continuously. Times and temperatures are checked and recorded. The chemical content of the iron ores received from the various mines are checked, and the ore is blended with other iron ore to achieve the desired charge. Samples are taken from each pour and checked for chemical content and mechanical properties such as strength and hardness.

f. Byproducts

The following by product as by product from the manufacturing process of iron.

***Pig iron*:** the molten iron withdrawn through a hole, slag hole, in to large lined with fire bricks which packed with tones of metal. The molten metal is cast into small semi cylindrical mould called pigs and hence the pig iron for the product.

***Furnace gases*:** The furnace gas which are on the mouth of furnace are 85% nitrogen, 25% carbon mono oxide, 10.5% Carbon dioxide and hydrogen ,lower hydrocarbons are about 6.5%.

g. Slag

Different types of impurities are collected as slag. There are many possible environmental effects from the iron industry. The first and most obvious is the process of open pit mining. Huge tracts of land are stripped to bare rock. Now days, depleted mining sites are commonly used as landfills, then covered over and landscaped. It is reported that some of these landfills themselves become environmental problems, since in the recent past; some were used for the disposal of highly toxic substances which leached into soil and water.

During the process of extracting iron from ore produces great quantities of poisonous and corrosive gases evolve. In practice, these gases are scrubbed and recycled. Inevitably, however, some small amounts of toxic gases escape to the atmosphere. A byproduct of iron purification is slag, which is produced in huge amounts. This material is largely inert, but must still be disposed of in landfills.

In the iron making huge amounts of coal is used . The coal is not used directly, but it is first reduced to coke which consists of almost pure carbon. The many chemical byproducts of coking are almost all toxic, but they are also commercially useful. These products include ammonia, phenol, cutting oils, cresols, pharmaceuticals, and photographic chemicals; and toluene are obtained.

Scrap iron and steel are also an environmental concern. Most of this material is recycled, however, since steel scrap is an essential resource in steel making. Scrap which isn't recycled eventually turns into iron oxide, or rust, and returns to the ground.

3. Allotropes of iron

Iron metal has been extracted from its ore around 2000 B.C. Pure iron being soft was rarely used. It was alloyed, mainly with carbon to obtain certain desired properties. Basically iron alloys have been divided into two forms, namely: cast iron and wrought iron. Iron alloys comprises of several solid phases.

There are several allotropic forms of iron. Ferrite or α-iron is stable up to 760°C. The change of β-iron involves primarily a loss of magnetic permeability because the lattice structure (body-centered cubic) is unchanged. The allotrope called γ-iron has the cubic close-packed arrangements of atoms and is stable from 910°C to 1400°C . Little is known about δ-iron except that it is stable above 1400°C and has a lattice similar to that of α-iron.

a. Ferrite

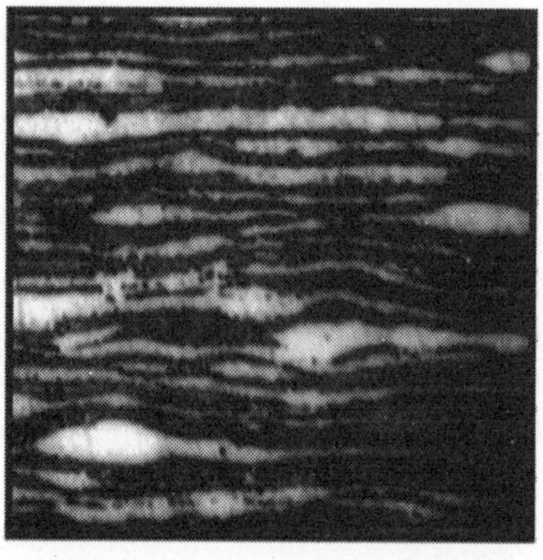

At room temperature, iron is in the form of ferrite, or α-iron, a body-centered cubic structure. It is the solid solution of carbon and other constituents. The density of α-iron is 7.86 g/cc. Distinction is made between low temperatures α ferrite with carbon solubility up to 0.02 percent and at high temperature δ ferrite.

Microstructure shows elongated ferrite and austenite grains. The ferrite and austenite is approximately in equal proportion with maximum carbon solubility of 0.1 percent. In the ferrite crystal lattice, the carbon atom is located in the center of the face of the cube where a sphere with the radius of 0.29R can be accommodated; R is the atomic radius of the iron. Carbon atoms are also located in the vacancies, on the dislocation. Under microscope ferrite may be seen as homogeneous polyhedral grains. It is a magnetic form of essentially pure iron nearly free from carbon but contains some elements as impurities like phosphorus, sulphur, silicon, etc. in varying amounts.

b. Austenite

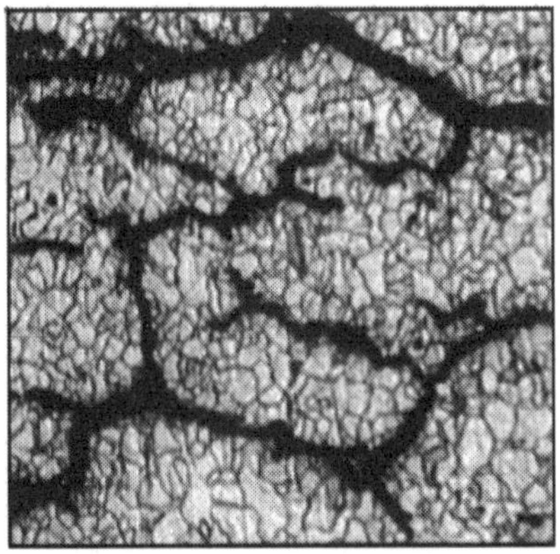

It is the solid solution of carbon and other constituents in γ-iron .The maximum solubility of carbon in γ-iron is 2.14 percent. At 910°C, it changes to γ-iron, which is face-centered cubic and somewhat softer. In γ-iron crystal lattice, carbon atom is located at the center of the unit cell, which can accommodate a sphere with radius of 0.41R.

Microstructure shows austenite grains with presence of heavy strain lines in the direction of rolling/forming. No carbide precipitation is seen.The different volume of the elementary sphere that can be accommodate in the body centered and face centered cubic lattice make carbon more soluble in γ-iron and α-iron. Austenite has high ductility and low yield tensile strengths. The microstructure is made up of polyhedral grains.

c. Cementite

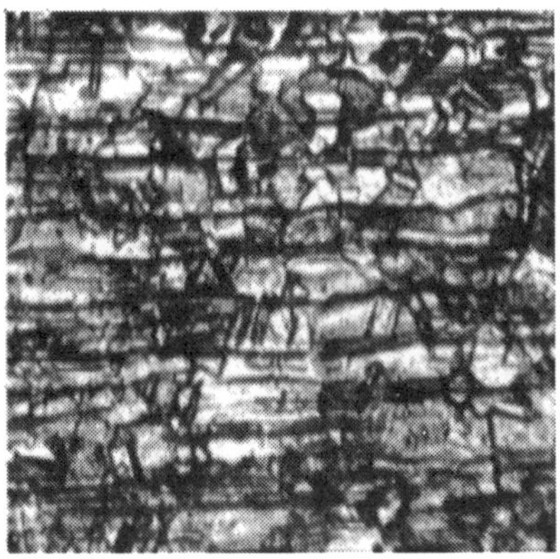

It is the chemical compound of carbon and iron. It consists of iron carbide as Fe_3C. An interesting aspect of iron chemistry and the array of compounds with bonds to carbon. It is a complex rhombic lattice with closed packed atoms. Owing to the possibility its decomposition, the melting point of the cementite has not been precisely determined, but it is equal to about 1550°C, cementite is ferromagnetic. The typical features of cementite are its high hardness and low ductility. Cementite is a meta stable phase .Under equilibrium condition, graphite is formed in alloy with high carbon content. Cementite, Fe_3C, is a component of steel. It is also found as a constituent of pearlite. It appears as a separate constituent in the grain boundaries of wrought iron containing about 0.02% carbon by weight .The rapid cooling partly or completely inhibits the crystallization of graphite and promotes the formation of cementite.

d. Pearlite

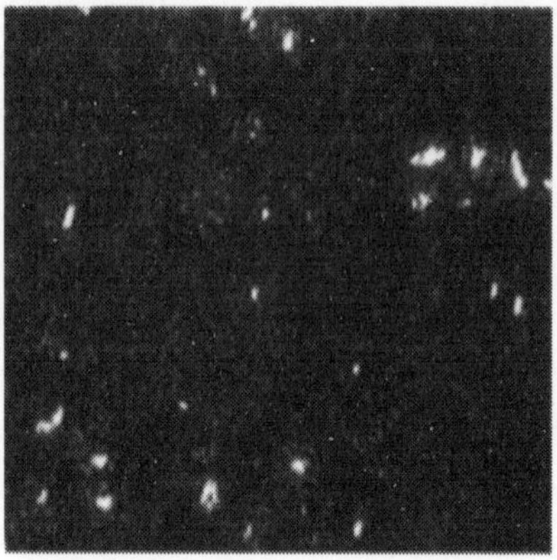

It is a mixture of ferrite and cementite usually in laminated form. Present in iron containing more than 0.02% carbon by weight and it is a product of slow cooling. When the temperature is reached at 727 °C, the carbon content of the austenite reaches 0.8%. The austenite of the eutectoid composition decomposes with the simultaneous of ferrite and cementite forming the pearlite.The more carbon in steel, the less the surplus ferrite and more the pearlite contains .It form the laminar structure but granular structure is form by the special heat treatment.

e. Graphite

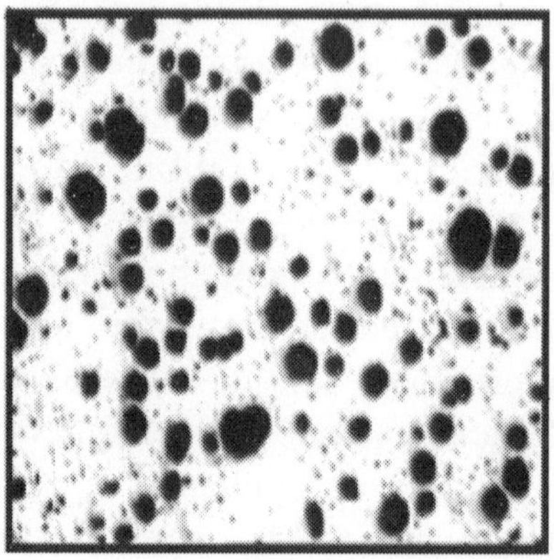

It is a form of carbon having a soft plate-like structure. It has a hexagonal layer lattice. The inter atomic spaces are small and equal to 1.4A° . Graphite is soft and has low strength and electrical conductivity. The carbon content of these phases increases from ferrite to pearlite to cementite to graphite, which is essentially pure carbon. The main reason iron did not show up in use earlier about 1500 BC was that it could not be melted or cast due to its very high melting point of 1537° C. The microstructure shows presence form in cast iron known as graphitization. If in the eutectic crystallization only graphite is separated out .The cast iron said to grey iron. If both graphite and cementite are separated out the cast iron said to be molted iron, if only cementite,it is said to be white cast iron.

f. Widmanstatten

In the wrought iron, relatively, some localized area having high carbon contentment .The pearlite and the ferrite are in the highly directional plate form in the localizes high carbon area. Widmanstatten structure may be unaffected at 400°C. The coarse area of pearlite and linear ferrite can be broken down to form of ferrite grains containing a random distribution of pearlite grains. This process is known as normalization of widmanstatten structure. These types of structure are formed after the 600 °C cycles and completely after the 1000 °C cycle.

4. Common useful forms of iron alloys (cast iron, wrought iron, and steel)

a. Wrought Iron

Wrought iron is made from cast iron by melting it on a bed of iron oxide. The final result get a material which is nearly pure iron, with only 0.1-0.2% of carbon and less than 0.5% of other impurities. The purification occurs in the iron because of iron oxide oxidizes the carbon to carbon monoxide and the sulphur, phosphorus and silicon to their oxides.

These oxides become part of the slag. As the iron becomes purer, its melting point rises and it becomes pasty, signaling the time to remove it from the furnace. The slag is then forced out by hammering. Normally wrought iron is a matrix of ferrite with slag inclusions. At the temperature of bellows' fires iron could be reduced to a spongy mass mixed with slag called bloom. Iron was manufactured either by direct process, bloom process or by conversion process such as pudding or fining up to 1500 A.D. With repeated hammering the blacksmith could drive out the slag to get a bar of almost pure iron. However, this iron had several bad properties- it was softer than bronze, did not hold a good edge, it rusted.

These processes do not involve more than 1250°C which is below than its melting point. Its means no liquid phase is involved and the reduction of ore to metal occurs in solid phase. As a result of this, the composition of the constituents throughout the alloy is not homogeneous. Therefore, though wrought iron is regarded as essentially pure iron, it is very heterogeneous with high and low carbon regions juxtaposed here and there but on the average it contains less than 0.1% carbon by weight. In the forged wrought iron, the slag are flattened and squeezed out along the working direction. This structure of normal wrought iron occurs in artifacts before 1900 AD. The modern wrought iron came in existence in 1900 AD.

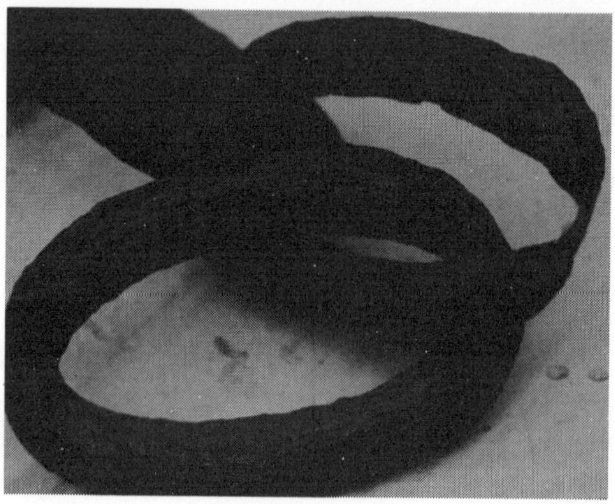

Wrought Iron Chain

When wrought iron fairly rapidly cooled from high temperature (1000°C) sometimes and containing more than 0.089% of carbon by weight then it acquires a metallurgical structure different from normal wrought iron. This structure is known as widmanstatten structure. The rapidly cooling is known as tempering: this involved two steps; quenching- which is the sudden cooling of hot metal by plunging it into water which makes it harder but somewhat brittle ,and after quenching re-heat it to about 700°C and then cool it to remove some of the brittleness and hardness. When working with bloom the charcoal and carbon monoxide produced by the fire will diffuse into the surface is known as steeling ; if carbon content 0.3% then it is better than bronze and the carbon content goes to 1.2% then it will be excellent iron in their property. The ejection of ferrite or cementite takes place along certain crystal planes forming a mesh like structure. The mesh like structure consists of discrete regions of relatively high carbon content and ferrite in the form of highly directional plates. Presence of some pearlite has also been observed. This structure was found to be absent in wrought iron manufactured after 1840 AD (North Owens and Pearson 1976: 92-197).

Wrought iron created by this process is strong and tough and can be welded and forged. Very popular in the past, it has now been largely supplanted by mild steel.

"Because they could not heat the iron to its melting point and cast it, this was to tie them to their anvils and frustrate mass production of iron goods for a thousand years."

b. Cast iron

Before 1000 years ago technique of manufacturing the cast iron was developed. There was used the melt iron with better furnaces due to achieved higher temperatures of the furnace and horizontal bellows and double acting box bellows and the burning of large amounts of high carbon fuel in relation to the amount of iron ore being smelted caused carbon monoxide to enter the iron and lower the melting point to about 1150° C.

These processes allows to cast iron. In this process melted iron is poured into molds. Cast iron is more brittle and must be made malleable. To do this heat the cast iron artifacts between 800 and 900° C in the presence of air. The oxygen removes some carbon from the surface which reduces some of the brittleness and forms a tough skin on the casting. Casting was found to be much easier to form original shapes.

In the 16th century AD the methods of casting of iron were developed. Cast iron is a generic name given to high carbon-iron alloys, which contain about 2-6% of carbon by weight and other elemental impurities such as silicon, phosphorus and sulphur in varying amounts.

The manufacture of cast iron involves liquid phase and it exists in two forms, (a) gray cast iron (b) white cast iron.

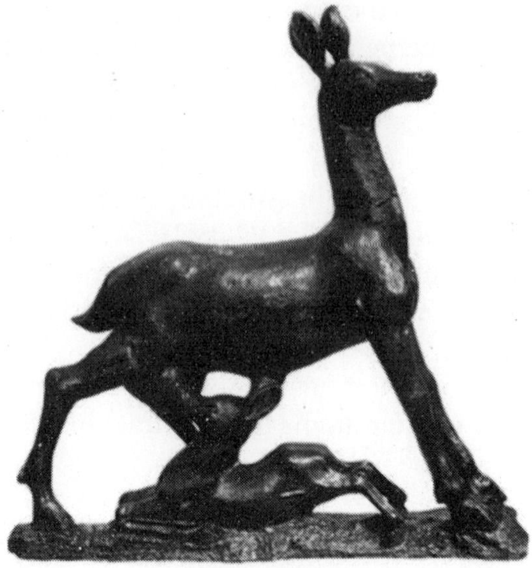

Cast iron sculpture

In the early artifacts white cast iron is more common. It contains low content of silicon, presence of manganese and sulphur and fast cooling favors the formation of white cast iron. To produce white cast iron from the gray cast iron chilling process has been used . It is extremely hard and brittle.

The cementite and pearlite are main phases in white cast iron. All carbon contains in this form of cast iron is found in cementite as "combined carbon".

Most of iron artifacts of the post 18th century are made up of grey cast iron. Slow cooling and presence of more than 1% silicon favors the formation of this type of cast iron. It contains about 3-4% carbon by weight and 1-3% silicon by weight. The ferrite, pearlite and graphite phases are present. The carbon exists mainly as graphite in the free form. When fractured, the exposed portion appears dull or grey because of the graphite. Flakes contained in its microstructure. Due to its excellent fluidity and relatively low melting point the grey cast iron can be easily cast into different shapes and forms. It shows brittleness due to lack of strength and the disposition of the graphite. It has no ductility

c. Iron steel

Steel is an alloy of iron and carbon with small amounts of other elements often present. Due to presence of carbon with small amounts of other elements therefore steel is much stronger and more flexible than iron. The greater the carbon content, the stronger and harder the steel, however, higher carbon content also makes the steel more brittle.

Steel is a purified alloy of iron with carbon which is manufactured in the liquid state. In the manufacturing process of steel eliminates almost all of the phosphorus, sulphur, and silicon which exist in common cast iron. The range of carbon content for steel is 0.1 to 1.5%. Low carbon steels (<0.2% carbon) are called mild steels. They are malleable and ductile and are used in place of wrought iron. Medium steels (0.2 to 0.45% carbon) are used for structural steel (beams, girders). Both mild and medium steels can be forged and welded. High-carbon steels (0.45 to 1.5% carbon) are used for making cutting tools, surgical instruments, drills and other tools. Medium and high-carbon steels can be hardened and tempered. Varying the amount of carbon and its distribution in the alloy controls the qualities of the resulting steel.

- Mild steel — 0.10% to 0 .25% carbon
- Medium carbon steel — 0.25% to 0 .45% carbon
- High carbon steel — 0.45% to 0 .95% carbon
- Ultrahigh carbon steel — 0.95% to 2.1% carbon

Ultra high carbon steel can be very brittle but with proper heat treating the strength of the steel may be maintained and the brittleness minimized. This process is known as tempering, and works in relationships as well as swords and knife. Some swords are made of layered metals of different steels. Softer more flexible steels are used on the inner layers and harder stronger steels for the outer layers. This creates a weapon that is flexible and holds a fine edge.

Stainless steel was first introduced in the early 1900s. Stainless steel is an iron alloy with chromium and other elements. Stainless steel is corrosion resistant steel. It is virtually immune to rust, discoloration, and corrosion. It can be highly polished resembling a precious metal. There are many different grades of stainless steel. Some grades can not hold an edge but when carbon is added to the alloy it can hold an edge.

d. Properties of Iron alloys

Iron is seldom pure and minor levels of other constituents can introduce very different properties into the resultant alloy.

Phosphorus	:	Harden and strengthen but makes it brittle when cold worked.
Sulphur	:	Introduces brittleness
Carbon	:	Ranging from 0-5% greatly affects the properties of the different alloys formed.

Some alloys of Iron :

	Alloys	*Metal added in %*	*Physical Properties*
•	Manganese steel.	2-15 Mn	Hard, tough, resistance to wear
•	Nickel steel	2.5-5.0 Ni	Hard, tough,rustless
•	Invar	3.6 Ni	Same coefficient of expansion as glass
•	Chrome steel	1.5-2 Cr	Extremely hard
•	Stainless Steel	13-14 Cr and1 Ni	Resist Corrosion
•	Tungsten Steel	14-20 tungsten	Hard and Strong
•	Chrome-Vanadium Steel	1.00 Cr, and 0.15	High tensile strength

There are found common phase of iron are soft ferrite means pure iron; hard brittle cementite means iron carbide and pearlite-laminations of ferrite and cementite, and graphite means pure carbon.

Iron formed by smelting is a spongy mass or bloom which can be consolidated into a solid lump by forging. When the bloom is heated in a reducing atmosphere in contact with carbon, as may happen during smelting, the iron on the surface becomes alloyed with carbon. When the lump is worked with an average of 0.1% carbon, the alloy areas become distributed throughout the artifact, resulting in a metal with an extremely heterogeneous composition. To raise deliberately the carbon content of an entire bloom by heating in this manner, the process is called carburization, is an extremely slow and expensive process requiring large amounts of charcoal. Thus in antiquity a tool or knife may have been fashioned from wrought iron and then only the working edges hardened by raising their content of carbon to about 0.3% through carburization, producing a steel zone. Other techniques of economically raising the carbon content of iron involve welding. Strips of carburized iron (steel) may be welded onto the cutting edge of a tool or weapon made from wrought iron.

To obtain an even distribution of steel throughout the artifact, it may be made from sheets or bars of carburized iron which are welded together and repeatedly forged to distribute the carbon compounds throughout artifact. This process is termed piling (Lamination) a more complicated method of increasing the mechanical strength to tools and weapons .This is the process of pattern welding: rods of iron are twisted into barleycorns, flattened and welded together. Grinding and polishing the surface of the resultant bars will produce a decorative pattern: this pattern and the increased strength may result from the incorporation of slag into the metal during forging.

Depending on their carbon content, iron alloys may be hardened still further by hammering. Steel owes its great usefulness to the enormous hardening derived when the alloy is rapidly cooled or quenched from 720°C, as a new very hard phase called martensite , is formed.

Iron made from primitive solid state by smelting which contain slag from the iron ore. The slags trapped within its pores. This mixture of glassy and crystalline faylite $2FeO.SiO_2$ is squeezed out to some degree by hammering. However, a certain percentage always remains in wrought iron and steel, drawn out in stringers along the line of working.

Cast iron, if made from liquid state smelting, is 'grey cast iron' as it contains flakes of black graphite. It is also contains high levels of phosphorous and silicon as impurities. White cast iron contains similarly high levels of carbon and carbon combines with iron to form cementite (FeC_3); its silicon level is lower than 'grey cast iron'. Both grey cast iron and white cast iron are extremely brittle and not workable, but they have much higher compressive strengths than wrought iron.

Recently investigation undergoing for the temperatures to which is safe to heat ancient iron without destroying metallurgical information. These would seem to be in the region of 380-400° C; prolonged heating at 100°C during treatment does not appear to bias archaemetallurgical studies.

Iron can be readily hot welded, it was used widely in antiquity; during welding the oxide is mechanically removed or fluxed off. This allows the joining not only of parts of an artifact but also of pieces of iron differing carbon contents allowing control over the properties of different areas within an artifact. Iron may also be joined by hard brazing spelter.It may be tinned for decorative or protective purposes, but tinning for the latter reason is only successful where the coating is perfect; or where the tin and iron are in very specific pH/E_H conditions; otherwise the iron where exposed, being more base than the tin, will corrode very rapidly by galvanic corrosion process. Before soldering or metal coatings are applied to iron, the surface must be well prepared and fluxes employed to counteract the marked tendency of iron to corrode and form obstructing oxide films.

CHAPTER-THREE

IRON ARTIFACTS

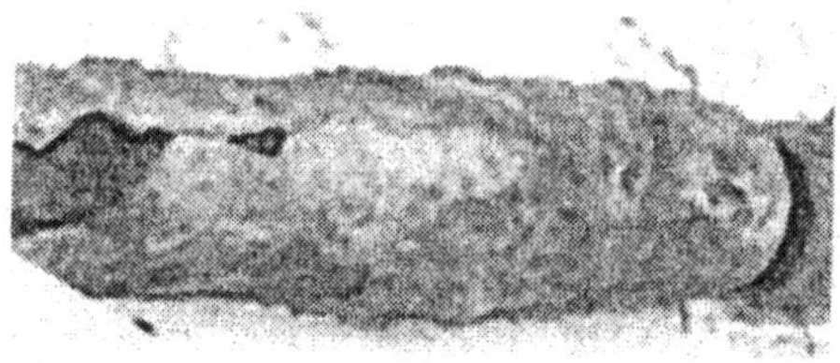

(Deterioration & Corrosion)

1. Deterioration and Corrosion of iron artifacts- an introduction

Deterioration is a universal and inevitable phenomenon which occurs in everything either that is living or non living in every climatic condition. It is a phenomenon which arises from the simultaneous effect of several causes. This statement applies not only to living things but also to the still object like iron artifacts.. There are various factors which contribute to its deterioration.

Corrosion is a chemical phenomenon in the favourable condition. In this phenomenon different type corrosion product is form depending upon environments and reactants. Here we will discus about the corrosion of iron.

Pure iron is a shiny, bright white, soft, malleable, ductile and strong metal. Its surface is usually discolored by corrosion and deterioration. Since it combines readily with the oxygen of the air in the presence of moisture. Actually in presence of absolute dry air iron does not rust. The oxides of the iron are formed in the presence of oxygen that is crumbly and soft, giving no protection to the base metal, which eventually rusts away. It is found in nature as the metal only in meteorites and in very rare circumstances where iron minerals have been reduced by environmental factors

Corrosion of iron is the deterioration of a material as a result of reaction with its surrounding environment, especially with oxygen and other reactants. Although the term is usually applied to metals, all materials deteriorate at the surface to some extent when they are exposed to certain combinations of liquids or gases. Common examples of metal corrosion are the rusting of iron, the dissolution of metals in the environment of acid solutions. Most research are involved into the causes and prevention of corrosion in metals, since the corrosion of metals occurs much faster under atmospheric conditions than the nonmetals. The maximum metal artifacts are destroyed by corrosion. In the case of artifacts they loose their identities and aesthetic values, which has carrying our past cultures.

2. Corrosion in soils burial iron artifacts

The corrosion mass is composed of iron oxides and carbonates in the main bulk of the corrosion product. The bulk may contain iron III Oxyhydroxides (FeO.OH).These bulk may be in the form of red,brown,yellow in the form of Goethite (αFeO.OH) and with some orange colour of Lepidocrocite (γFeO.OH).But there can also be considerable quantities of amorphous Limonite(FeO.OH), Siderite (Fe CO_3) and calcium carbonate on iron in the calcareous soils. Pale buff, yellow powdery is Jarosite a basic iron (III) sulphate ($NaFe_3(OH)_6(SO4)_2$). By controlled heating of iron deliberately blue, black or brown colour oxide are formed ; brown patinas may be form naturally in relatively pollutionless dry air . However, humidity and the presence of corrosion stimulators will normally cause such a oxide to develop into a thicker crust of minerals. The conversion of the iron artifact in main minerals in the soils burial artifacts are:

	Mineral	*Formula*	*Colour of mineral*
1.	Goethite	α-FeO(OH)	Red/ Brown/yellow
2.	Lepidocrocite	γFeO(OH)	Orange
3.	Limonite	FeO(OH)	Amorhous, can't protect metal underneath
4.	Jarosite	$NaFe_3(OH)_6$ $(SO4)_2)$	Pale buff, Yellow Powdery (Basic Fe-III Sulphate)
5.	Hematite	$\alpha Fe_2 O_3$	Red Yellow
6.	Vivianite	$Fe_3(PO4)_2.8H_2O$.	Blue, black (iron phosphate)
7.	Siderite	$(FeCO_3)$	
8.	Iron (iii) Oxy-hydroxides	FeO.OH	

Brick bright red compact colour layer of hematite (αFe_2O_3) is formed when iron is heated above 200°C and it prevents further corrosion for a considerable time. This is an extremely protective layer. Such a layer may be found within a corrosion crust when the protection of the haematite has been broken down. In the some cases of archaeological iron artifacts, haematite could be indicating the burning of material surrounding the iron before it was buried.

The black colouration on the iron artifacts from wet oxygen environment the free deposits often appear black because of iron (ii) sulphide formed by sulphate reducing bacteria. This layer can be hard and shiny or sludge like with the metal. Bright blue to blue black colouration of the Vivianite (iron phosphate) which is in the form of Fe-II phosphate ($Fe_3(PO4)_2.8H_2O$).Covering of Vivianite are found in artifacts from wet organic layers or from a phosphate rich area. Oxygenated organic deposits can form blue black coatings of phenolic iron complexes (T. Stembolov-125). On the some occasions it is found that heavily corroded iron artifacts are stable after excavation, but it is more usual to find that after some weeks or years, lumps or as cleaned iron corrosion product pseudomorphs begins to disintegrate. The artifact splits up in the case of wrought iron along the direction of working, to reveal damp, dark orange brown spots.

It has been noted that artifacts which still retain metallic iron even though this is only vestigial, are those which are most likely to break up the totally corroded or hollow artifacts often appear stable.

3. Corrosion of Iron in Marine Environment

In the marine environment the surface of concretion is occasionally covered by a thin white or pale brown crust, but more often it is coated with a loose deposit of rusty corrosion products .These outer layers contain a high proportion of calcium, magnesium carbonate, hydroxide and also Siderite (Fe CO_3), but inside they consist almost entirely of the oxides and hydrated oxides of iron. Silica (SiO_2) and black iron sulphide (FeS) may also occur. Concretions found within marine sediment, where oxygen is relatively scarce, contain higher proportions of Lepidocrocite (γFeO.OH), Black Magnetite (Fe_3O_4), Magnetic Sulphide, Pyrorrhotite, other compounds which are unstable in marine atmospheric conditions and difficult to identify are also be present.

The corroded marine wrought iron is more likely to land sites corroded wrought iron. Its tends to corrode along the lines of the slag stringers it contains. Where it is exposed often has a fibrous surface which resembles wood. Black concretion of the cast iron is likely to retain its shape under such conditions, wrought iron may well disappear completely. Green concretion of the iron due to green rust a mixture of iron (II) and iron (III) hydrated oxides found on cast and wrought iron but it also found on artifacts from landsite excavated iron artifacts.

The conversion of the iron artifact in main minerals in marine environment

Mineral	*Formula*	*Colour of mineral*
1. Lepidocrocite	γFeO.OH	Orange
2. Magnetite	Fe3O4	Black
3. Limonite	FeO.OH	Amorhous, can't protect metal underneath
4. Siderite	$FeCO_3$	
5. Iron sulphide	Fe S	Black

4. Terminology in Corrosion

Iron artifacts are more prone to corrosion in the favorable condition and try to reach in the mineralized state. Before discussion on the corrosion process on iron and iron artifacts the discussion on some terminology used in the corrosion process is necessary:

Crystal	:	A type of solid in which the particles are arranged in a definite geometric lattice; the basic cell, reproduced in three-dimensional space, results in one of fourteen commonly found crystal types.
Alloys	:	Materials made by melting together two or more elements, at least one of which is a metal.eg.steel, manganese steel, Nickel steel, Invar ,Chrome steel, Stainless Steel ,Tungsten Steel and Chrome-Vanadium Steel.
Anode	:	A site of chemical oxidation or loss of electrons.
Cathode	:	A site of chemical reduction or gain of electrons.
Corrosion	:	A destructive chemical process; most often applied to the conversion of a metal to one of its compounds, for example, the corrosion of iron by oxygen and water to produce iron oxides (rust).
Electrolysis	:	A substance that exists in water as ions; the resulting solution can carry an electrical current.
Electromotive series	:	A tabulation of the metals in order of tendency to be oxidized or reduced.
Redox reaction	:	A chemical reaction in which one reactant is oxidized or loses electrons while another is reduced or gains electrons.
Corrosion Products	:	A layer of corrosion products that forms on the surface of a corroding metal; the cover may or may not form a barrier to further attack.

5. The role of Electromotive series in corrosion of the iron artifacts

All metal exhibits a tendency to be oxidized more easily than others, knowledge of metal location in a series is an important piece of information to have making decision about its potential usefulness for structural and other applications. We can explain in short in the case of corrosion of metal like iron which is more easily corroded than others. This is due to existence of cathodic and anodic sites on the surface of iron artifact and implies that differences in electrical potential on the surface. Due to this potential difference there have a number of defects. The Standard reduction potentials in salt solutions of normal ionic activity at 20°C and pH = 0.

Noble End (Cathodic)	*Ionic Reaction Electrode Potential*
1. Gold (+1 aurous, +3 auric)	$Au^{+3} + 3e^{-} \leftarrow \rightarrow Au$ +1.50
2. Silver (+1)	$Ag^{+} + e^{-} \leftarrow \rightarrow Ag$ +.799
3. Copper (+1 cuprous)	$Cu^{+} + e^{-} \leftarrow \rightarrow Cu$ +0.552
4. Copper (+2 cupric)	$Cu^{+2} + 2e^{-} \leftarrow \rightarrow Cu$ +0.337
5. Hydrogen (+1)	$2H^{+} + 2e^{-} \leftarrow \rightarrow H_2$ +0.0
6. Lead (+2 plumbus, +4 plumbic)	$Pb^{+2} + 2e^{-} \leftarrow \rightarrow Pb$ -0.126
7. Tin (+2 stannous, +4 stannic)	$Sn^{+2} + 2e^{-} \leftarrow \rightarrow Sn$ -0.136
8. Iron (+2 ferrous)	$Fe^{+2} + 2e^{-} \leftarrow \rightarrow Fe$ -.440 -0.409
9. Iron (+3 ferric)	$Fe^{+3} + 3e^{-} \leftarrow \rightarrow Fe$ -0.036
10. Zinc (+2)	$Zn^{+2} + 2e^{-} \leftarrow \rightarrow Zn$ -0.763
Base End (Anodic)	

6. Corrosion of Wrought iron and Cast Iron

Wrought iron tends to corrode by loss of metal from the surface in a moist oxygenated environment thereafter corrosion process proceeds in a front which moves down into the metal more or less parallel to the surfaces. Below the outer rust the black coloured oxide magnetite (Fe_3O_4) is form in region of low oxygen. Where corrosion is completed and iron is replaced entirely by black dense lustrous magnetite underlying a greater or lesser zone of brown oxides. The original surface can be detected by careful investigation and cleaning. The original surface can be seen as a denser zone of corrosion which unlike the overlying bulk. It does not incorporate grains of sand and other materials. In the certain moist oxygenated deposits on wrought iron artifacts, which occur both in the sea and on the land sites, it is found that all the oxidized iron of an iron artifact has migrated into the surrounding environment and small wrought iron artifact may disperse completely within many years. Unlike wrought iron, cast iron from the marine sites is always remains solid, even totally corroded and encased within a crust of ferrous concretion. The surface of the corroded artifact is very soft and often consists of a matrix of rusty corrosion products with small lustrous inclusions under the crust. These are flakes of graphite of grey cast iron which survive, having been the cathodic part of an iron-carbon galvanic corrosion cell, while the base iron corrodes preferentially. The iron oxide and carbonates formed in situ between metal and graphite flakes is preserved. In the cast iron, similar internal galvanic corrosion cells form between the metal and the more noble areas of cementite, and again the original shape of the artifact is preserved.

Corrosion is caused by chemical reaction with the environment, affects materials as different as structural metal artifacts from past civilizations. Corrosion technology is a field of study that focuses on the mechanisms of corrosion and on the design of protective schemes to prevent it or limit its extent. Corrosion is an electrochemical process in which corroding metal behaves like a small electrochemical cell. The corrosion of iron is a important redox reaction by dissolved oxygen, occurring in that environment. For example an iron artifact exposed to a water solution containing dissolved oxygen acts as one site of oxidation and other site reduction half-reactions, which occur at different locations on the surface. Iron is oxidized at anodic areas and on the same time oxygen molecules in the solution are reduced at the cathodic areas. These two processes produce an insoluble ferrous hydroxide $Fe(OH)_2$ in the first step of the corrosion process.

Thereafter this iron hydroxide is further oxidized in a second step to produce ferric hydroxide $Fe (OH)_3$, the flaky, reddish-brown substance that is known as rust. This new compound ferric hydroxide $(FeOH)_3$ is permeable to oxygen and water, so it does not form a protective coating on the iron surface and the corrosion process continues.

Metals have oxidizing tendency. A table of the relative strength of metals oxidizing tendency is called the electromotive series. Knowledge of a particular metal's location in the electromotive series of metals is an important piece of information to have in making decisions about its potential usefulness for structural and other applications.

The existence of anodic and cathodic sites on the surface of a piece of metal implies that differences in electrical potential are found on the surface. The potential differences are due to the important mechanism of oxygen concentration cell corrosion, in which the oxygen concentration in the electrolyte varies from place to place. An underground metal that passes from clay to gravel will have a high oxygen concentration in the gravel region and almost no oxygen in the impermeable clay. The part of the iron in contact with the clay becomes anodic and suffers damage. The cure for this is cathodic protection, which involves the use of a sacrificial anode such as zinc or aluminum. In this situation, the metal to be protected is connected electrically to a piece of scrap metal that will take its place as the anode. The anode is destroyed by the corrosion reaction, leaving the cathode intact. This technique is still used extensively to protect underground iron.

Although most metals are crystalline in form and generally they are not in continuous single crystals, but rather they are collections of small grains or domains in localized order. Metal artifacts are formed from melts in which micro crystals formed as the liquid cooled and solidified. Finally these micro crystals have different orientations with respect to one another. The edges of the domains form grain boundaries, which are an example of planar defects in metals. These planner defects are usually sites of chemical reactivity. The boundaries become anodic, while the grains themselves are the cathodes. The boundaries have weaknesses, the places where stress cracking begins.

All types of corrosion is galvanic corrosion, which occurs at the contact point of two metals or alloys with different electrode potentials. An obvious area of concern is the iron artifacts welds to fuse together pieces of another metal. The combination to be desired is the large anode-small cathode combination. Any artifact should be made of the metal less likely to be oxidized so that the artifact or weld portion is catholically protected.

The conductivity of the corroding solution has the great importance. Whenever the large area of the surface are in contact with a water solution of high conductivity, such as seawater, the attack on the anodic metal may spread far from its contact point with the cathodic metal. This is a less severe situation than that which occurs in soft water or under atmospheric conditions in which the attack is localized in the vicinity of the contact. Galvanic corrosion does not occur in the absence of dissolved oxygen or hydrogen ions. Since to maintain the cathode process nothing is present in the solution. It is possible to combine different metals with little corrosion. Iron being a higher energy level is thermodynamically unstable. Therefore, they tend to liberate free energy to achieve in the stable states. Corrosion is a chemical or electrochemical process in which a metal is converted to its mineral forms. Theoretically corrosion should proceed in iron until no metal core is remains. But in reality it seldom goes to such an extent, because of the inter-relationship between various factors controlling corrosion.

Corrosion of metals is basically aqueous corrosion and the mechanism involved is electrochemical. The electro chemical reactions are of two types

Anodic reactions: where oxidation of metal takes places at the anodic site.

Cathodic reactions: where the reduction of oxygen or hydrogen evolution takes place at the cathodic site.
It may be represented as:

$$M \rightarrow M^{+} + ne \qquad \text{anodic reaction}$$

$$O_2 + 2H_2O + 4e^{-} \rightarrow 4OH^{-} \qquad \text{cathode reactions.}$$

$$2H^{+} + 2e \rightarrow H_2$$

At the anodic site, iron ions leave the solid metal surface and go into the electrolyte, leaving the electron(s) into the metal. These electrons flow through the bulk of the metal to the cathodic site where they are used up in the cathodic reactions, thus completing the electronic circuit, and at the same time restoring the charge balance in the metal (P.J. Gellings1985 and A .John Sedriks 1979). In the electrolyte the addition of positive charges (metal irons) is counter-balanced by the formation of negative charges (hydroxyl ions) or removal of H^+ ions (H_2 evolution) at the cathodic sites.

Sometimes due to the development of high resistance between the anodes and cathodes, polarization of these electrodes result, i.e. electrons accumulate at the anodic area, making it more negative while, due to electron deficiency the cathodic areas become more positive. The rate of corrosion became slow down due to this cause. So, for proceed to corrosion there must be movement of reactants and products to and fro.

Iron ions can be removed by diffusion into the surrounding electrolyte solution by formation of insoluble precipitates or by combination with other species to form complex ions. Cathodic depolarization may be achieved by availability of dissolved oxygen. Corrosion being a redox reaction, its may be expressed by the reduction potential or corrosion potential of the metal.

Iron is usually the most prevalent metal in archeological sites. During conservation and preservation of iron artifacts at archeological sites , conservator should be present because the variety of conditions and environments under which corrosion can occur and due to the numbers and complexities of the corrosion products. Moreover, corrosion processes are applicable to other metals and make iron a useful introduction to all metallic corrosion. It is discussed in more detail and is used to introduce and define electrochemical corrosion(Evans 1961, Potter 1956:236-237, Pourbaix 1966, Hamilton 1976, and Pearson 1987a).

7. Mechanism of Electrochemical Corrosion

Iron buried in the soils or lying on the ground surface exposed only to ground and air moisture corrodes essentially by an electrochemical process. The corrosion of iron in marine water proceeds in somewhat the same manner but is greatly accelerated because normally water becomes more corrosive as the salt content increases. For example, iron corrodes five times faster in marine water than in soil and ten times faster in marine water than in air (Cornet 1970).

Iron artifacts buried in the soils and ground, pitting is generally a prominent feature of the corrosion process, and this environment tends to be chemically reducing and forming soluble ferrous ions which often diffuse some distance away from the iron surface. When iron is buried in an aerobic soil or exposed on the surface to the air, the ferrous ions initially formed in the corrosion process oxidize to ferric ions which results in layers of ferric oxide scale on the iron artifact surface. This ferric oxide scale tends to form layers that may crack and spell due to the differences in the thermal expansion coefficients between the ferrous and ferric corrosion products and iron. Alternatively, the corrosion products may inhibit additional corrosion because they form a protective film. Air-oxidized artifacts occupy more volume than the original iron artifact, and usually have obvious layers of ferric oxide scale. If salts, such as sodium chloride, are present in the water, or in the soil, a very conductive solution is formed and electrochemical corrosion is accelerated. In electrochemical corrosion a galvanic cell can be created when two different metals, or different areas on the same metal, are coupled by means of an electrical or ion-conducting electrolyte. The result is an electrochemical reaction. In essence, electrochemical corrosion is reserved for those processes where a current flows between anodic and cathodic areas situated at different parts of a metallic surface or between two different metals of the same or different material. The formation of ferrous ions as the initial corrosion product in the electrochemical oxidation of iron.

The corrosion of submerged metals in salt water, as in the case of shipwrecks, is a complex process. It has often been explained in terms of a large galvanic cell (Peterson 1969; 1972) .Which is based on the electromotive series of metals. It may state in general terms that all the metals are compared in an electrochemical cell with a hydrogen electrode, which is given an arbitrary electrode value of zero. Metals that have a potential more negative than hydrogen in a galvanic cell are said to have a negative electrode potential and metals having a potential more positive to hydrogen have a positive electrode potential. By measuring the electromotive force (EMF) in volts required to balance a galvanic cell formed by a particular metal immersed in a solution of its salts of normal cation activity and a hydrogen electrode, the metals are arranged according to their relative chemical activity or electrode potential into an electromotive series of the metals . The least active metals are placed at the top and the most active ones are placed at the bottom. The more negative the electrode potential is the more active the metal and have a greater tendency for the atoms to lose electrons and form positive ions which under go into solution. The ions of metal go into solution. The parent metal always becomes negatively charged, regardless of its electrode potential sign. When two metals form an electrochemical cell, the metal having the more negative reduction electrode potential in the electromotive series becomes the anode. It loses electrons and forms positive ions which go into solution. The more noble or positive metal in the cell forms the cathode and is given cathodic protection, while the anodic metal is preferentially corroded in any resulting electrochemical reaction.

The corrosion and large mass of different metals in salty water is on the basis of the large galvanic cell concept and the electromotive position of the metals have been overplayed which are not completely understood. The large mass of different metals associated with a sunken ship in salt water consists of thousands of independent galvanic cells and does not form a single gigantic battery. Each galvanic cell is formed between two metals having different electrode potentials. In order to establish a galvanic cell the metals have to be in very close proximity or in contact. This requirement necessarily limits the metals that can form a galvanic couple to a single encrustation. Even then, different variables such as conductivity of the electrolyte, aggressive ion concentration, and mass transport can come into play and alter or interfere with the expected theoretical.

The electrochemical corrosion of metals has been detailed in a number of sources. In the case of iron, it has been shown by Evans (1963:28) and Potter (1956:236-237) that in any electrochemical cell where iron establishes a metallic couple in salt water with a more noble metal, it may be copper or silver, or even another piece of iron or a different part of the same iron artifact, the anodic and cathodic reactions are the same. At the surface of the more noble metal the cathode is formed. The reaction is may be shown as:

$$2H_2O \rightarrow 2H^+ + 2OH^-$$
$$2H^+ + 2e \rightarrow H_2\uparrow$$

The hydroxides combine with the sodium ion in the solution to form sodium hydroxide as the cathodic product.

$$NaCl \rightarrow Na^+ + Cl^-$$
$$Na^+ + OH^- \rightarrow NaOH$$

At the anode the reaction is the production of ferrous ions, which in turn combines with chloride in the salt water to form ferrous chloride as the anodic product.

$$Fe - 2e^- \rightarrow Fe^{+2}$$
$$Fe^{+2} + 2Cl^- \rightarrow FeCl_2$$

On exposure to air or solutions containing dissolved oxygen, the ferrous chloride oxidizes to ferric chloride and ferric oxide. Sodium hydroxide, ferrous chloride, and ferric chloride are freely soluble and may yield ferrous hydroxide where they meet.

$$FeCl_2 + 2NaOH \rightarrow Fe(OH)_2 + 2NaCl$$

The solutions containing dissolved oxygen a secondary take place reaction oxidizes the ferrous hydroxide to a ferric state. In the presence of hydroxyl ions in a neutral or slightly alkaline solution, this hydrated ferric hydroxide (any form of ferric oxide with internal water, i.e., common rust) is precipitated on or about the electrodes of the cell. The sequence of reaction at an iron anode in the presence of oxygen as stated by Potter (1956:236-237) is:

$$Fe - 2e \rightarrow Fe^{+2} \quad \text{Ferrous ion}$$
$$Fe^{+2} + 2OH^- \rightarrow Fe(OH)_2 \quad \text{Ferrous hydroxide}$$

Hydrated ferric hydroxide is red-brown rust is form by the reaction of oxygen on ferrous hydroxide.

$$4Fe(OH)_2 + O_2 \rightarrow 2H_2O + 2Fe(OH)_3.H_2O$$

The primary anodic reaction of electrochemical corrosion of iron is the production of ferrous ions. The secondary stage, the oxidation of the ferrous ion compounds to a ferric state, is modified when the supply of oxygen is restricted as in stagnant water or in the soil. Intermediate oxidation products of ferrous hydroxide such as hydrated magnetite and black magnetite are formed (Evans 1963:28; Potter 1956:236-237).

$6Fe(OH)_2 + O_2 \rightarrow 4H_2O + 2Fe_3O_4.H_2O$ (Green hydrated magnetite)
$Fe_3O_4.H_2O \rightarrow H_2O + Fe_3O_4$ (Black magnetite)

Depending on the environment, the corrosion products can take on a variety of physical forms, state of division, and hydration. It is common to find corroded iron with an outer layer of hydrated ferric hydroxide (common rust) which has restricted the supply of oxygen to the ferrous hydroxide briefly formed at the surface of the metal. Laminated corrosion layers consisting of an inner layer of black magnetite, a thin layer of hydrated magnetite and an outer layer of hydrated ferric hydroxide are formed.

$Fe(OH)_3.H_2O$	Hydrated Ferric hydroxide
$Fe_3O_4.H_2O$	Hydrated magnetite
Fe_3O_4	Black magnetite

In the electrochemical cell the electrodes could consist of two different pieces of the same metal or different parts of the same artifact. This may be clarify that metals are exceptionally pure, so that a metallic surface is almost to contain certain inclusions . Due to this reason a metal need not be in contact with a more noble metal to corrode in water. An oxide scale layer on a metal surface will be cathodic to the metal which will be anodic in the presence of an electrolyte. A metallic couple between the two can form a number of galvanic cells. Electrochemical cells may also form on a chemically homogeneous metal in areas of mechanical stress, such as a dent or a bend, and concentrate the corrosion along this stress line. The stress corrosion is a very important factor in the corrosion and deterioration of iron artifacts. Even if a metal is pure without an oxide layer or area of stress, immersion in a solution such as sea water which contains traces of salts of noble metals can cause the formation of local cells at the metal surface which effectively corrode the iron artifact (Potter 1956:238; Leigh 1973:20). The effects of variation in oxygen concentration, temperature, and pH at a metal surface will cause corrosion.

It is interesting point that how two different areas of the same metal can become anodic and cathodic to form an electrolytic cell. The flow of the electrons to the cathodic area from the anodic area causing the metal to corrode by forming soluble positive ions at the anode. Millions of these type of cells are formed over the surface of the metal and result is massive oxidation and it is continue until get an equilibrium state. The corrosion process is halted at the cells when they come into equilibrium but may continue at alternate anodic and cathodic positions on the artifact until the bulk of the metal is oxidized. According to the principles of electrochemistry, iron oxidizes preferentially in a galvanic cell with iron as one electrode and copper or silver as the other electrode. There are many variables, such as surface area, electrolyte and mass transport, play a role in the corrosion process. All variables have to be considered when an artifact with a great array of organic and metallic material is deposited in salt water. A major factor to be considered is that, as the metals corrode in salt water, there are localized changes in the pH which upset the equilibrium between the dissolved calcium carbonate and dissolved carbon dioxide in the sea water (Leigh 1973:205). There are precipitates of insoluble calcium carbonate and magnesium hydroxide. This insoluble calcium carbonate and magnesium hydroxide and the corrosion products especially ferrous hydroxide, ferrous sulphide, and magnetite are intermixing with sand and marine life to form a hard dense layer of encrustation or concretion around the metal. The encrustation accumulates on the original metal surface to form a perfect mold around the artifact. The encrustations can actually separate two metal pieces that are initially touching each other and prevent galvanic corrosion. While processing artifacts from a number of archaeological site those are indeed a rare occurrence to ever find any two metal artifacts actually touching each other. They are always separated by a layer of encrustation. Such encrustation effectively separates the metals from each other and destroys the electrochemical cell by cutting off the current flow and oxygen supply.

8. Anaerobic Corrosion

The corrosion processes are impeded by the formation of the surrounding encrustation. The deterioration becomes continues because of the presence of sulphate-reducing bactria and these bacteria play an important role as large part in the corrosion of iron in salt water, in fresh water and buried in the soil under anaerobic conditions (Evans 1963:224; Leigh 1973:205; Pearson 1972:35). It has been acknowledged that the various species of these bacteria play an important and large role in the chemical corrosion of iron in waterlogged anaerobic environments. In fact, as much as 60% of the corrosion of iron in salt water can be attributed to bacterial action (Pearson 1972:35). On accounts for most of the rapid corrosion of buried iron in waterlogged clay soils , the bacteria is most responsible. Sulphate-reducing bacteria, particularly the strains known as Sporovibrio desulphuricans and Desulphovibrio desulphuricans are commonly found in salt water, fresh water, and waterlogged soil (Pearson 1972:35) (Farrer, et al. 1953:82). Localized anaerobic environments created by the decaying organic material in sea water which has a large supply of sulphates and consumes oxygen .Under aerobic conditions these bacteria utilize hydrogen to reduce the sulphates (SO_4^{-2}) to sulphides (S^{-2}) as a metabolic by-product according to the reaction:

$$H_2SO_4 + 8H \rightarrow H_2S + 4H_2O$$

In this process the hydrogen that accumulates on the iron as a cathodic product polarizes the cathode in an oxygen-free environment. The polarization of the cathode is ordinarily halts in the electrochemical corrosion process. However, the utilization of hydrogen in the metabolism of the bacteria depolarizes the cathodic areas of the cell and allows the corrosion to continue unabated. The hydrogen sulphide formed as a metabolic by-product and it reacts not only with iron, but all the metals of antiquity except gold and accelerates the corrosion process. The hydrogen sulphide reacts with the ferrous ion from the anodic areas to produce ferrous sulphide and ferrous hydroxide, two major corrosion compounds of iron (Leigh 1973). The corrosion process in iron by Pearson 1972 assumption are as follows:

$$Fe^{+2} + H_2S \rightarrow FeS + 2H^+ \quad \text{Ferrous sulphide}$$
$$3Fe^{+2} + 6OH^- \rightarrow 3Fe(OH)_2 \quad \text{Ferrous hydroxide}$$
$$4Fe + H_2SO_4 + 2H_2O \rightarrow FeS + 3Fe(OH)_2 \quad \text{overall reaction}$$

The life cycle of the sulphate-reducing bacteria stimulates both the cathodic and anodic reactions of the electro-chemical corrosion process. In some cases, however, the precipitation of a continuous film or layer of iron sulphide may stifle rather than stimulate the anodic reaction (Evans 1963:225). Without the presence of sulphate-reducing bacteria, the corrosion of iron and other metals in anaerobic environments would be effectively inhibited.

9. Corrosion of Ferrous Alloys

It has been found that there is comparatively little difference in the corrosion of mild steel, wrought iron, and numerous low alloy steels(Evans 1963). Even cast iron oxides by the same processes including the action of sulphate-reducing bacteria. When cast iron is submerged in salt water, it undergoes a corrosion process called graphitization (Patoharju 1964:316, 1973:10; Pearson 1972:10). In this reaction the salt water conducts a current between the anodic pearlite in the iron and the cathodic graphite flakes to form a galvanic cell. The pearlite corrodes, leaving a porous framework of graphite filled with the iron corrosion products. This graphite framework can maintain the original form of the artifact with little outward change in appearance, but there would be considerable loss of density and mechanical strength. The process can proceed until the bulk of the metallic iron has corroded within the graphite framework. Ultimately deformation has to result because the graphite framework is not capable of supporting the artifact by itself.

10. Types of Corrosion

i. General and Uniform Corrosion

In this type of corrosion the anodic areas on metal surface shift to different positions until at some time the entire surface have been anodic. All areas of the metal surface corrode at the same rate, this being characterized by progressive and uniform thinning of the metal component.

ii. Pitting Corrosion

On the metal surface the anodic area are form on the surface .The anodie remain confined to certain discrete regions, resulting in the formation of pits and cavities. Corrosion penetrates into the metal, sometimes leading to perforation due to cyclic process. It is strongly localized type corrosion. Pitting corrosion occur with passive metals. Pit initiation may have different causes such as mechanical damage, heterogeneities, local cold working of the metal,deposite of dirt, differences in composition of the environment.

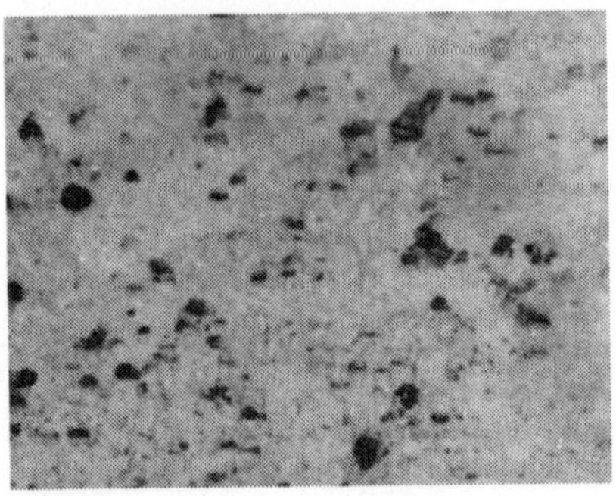

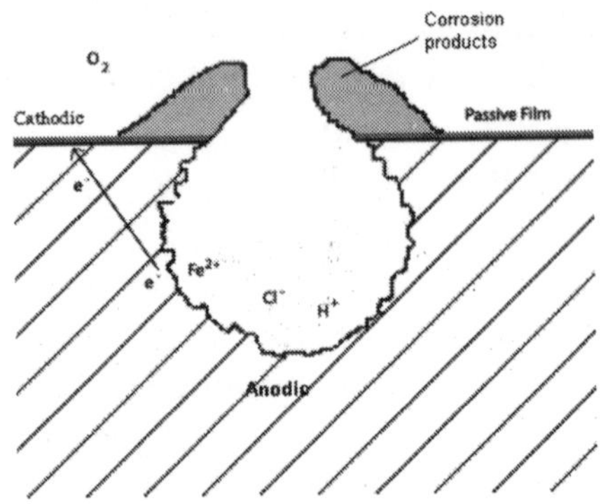

iii. Galvanic Corrosion

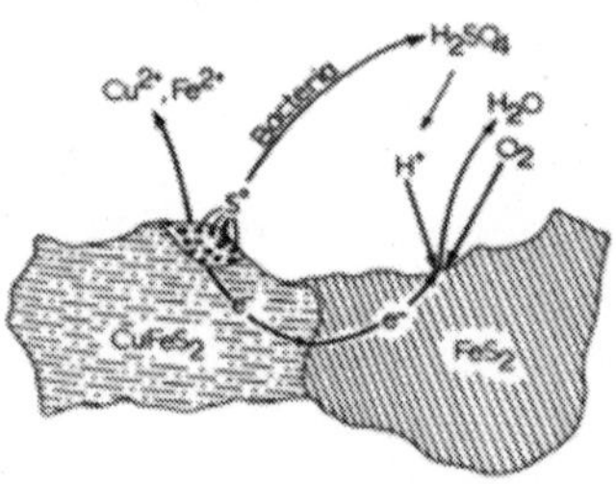

A galvanic cell is set up between two dissimilar metals, having different electrode potentials and are in electrical contact with each other in the presence of an electrolyte. The metal having lower electrode potential will corrode in preference to the one with higher electrode potential.

iv. Stress Corrosion

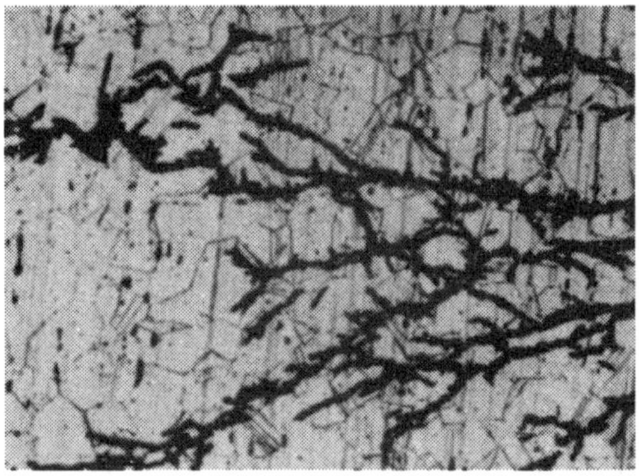

This type of electrochemical corrosion arises due to the presence of physical strains in the crystal structure of the metal. It is developed during the cold working process. Accelerated corrosion occurs at the internally stressed sites, often resulting in the metal cracking.

v. Erosion Corrosion

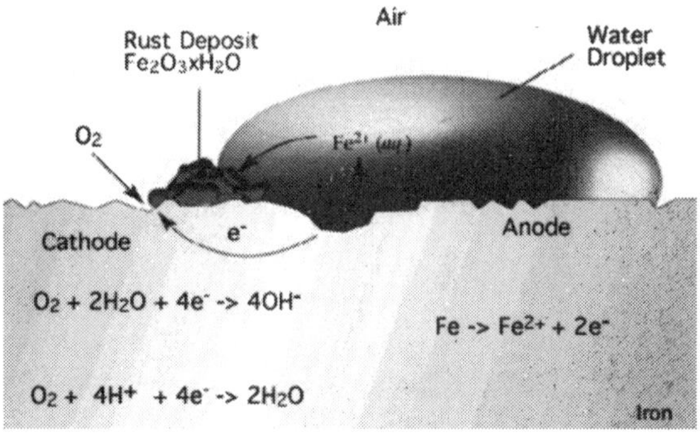

It is the accelerated rate of corrosion due to the relatively rapid movement of the metal surface and its surrounding environment. Metal surface suffers loss of cations as well as solid corrosion products, which are mechanically removed from the surface by the abrasives and rapidly flowing of abrasive environment.

vi. Inter-granular / grain boundary corrosion

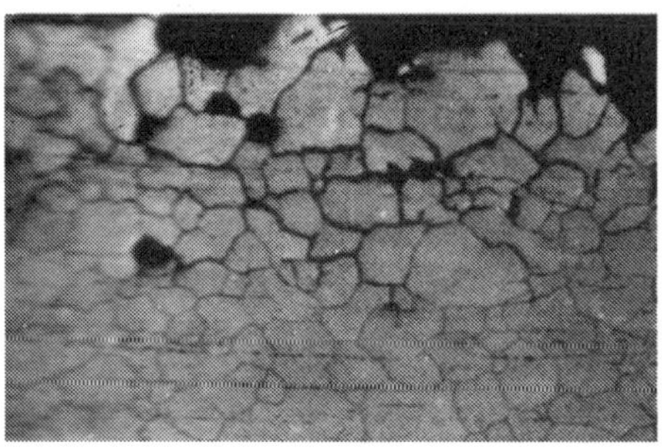

All metals are polycrystalline. They are consist of a large number of small, usually randomly oriented ,crystalline region known as crystallite or grains. The inter-granular or grain boundary corrosion is a form of electrochemical corrosion occurring along the grain-boundaries of a metal. The periphery of the grain becomes anodic while the center of the grain becomes cathodic. The damage may be mainly internal resulting in initial disintegration of the metal components. Usually starts on metal surface, proceeding rapidly to the bulk of the metal. This type of corrosion in austenic stainless steels.

vii. Concentration Cell Corrosion

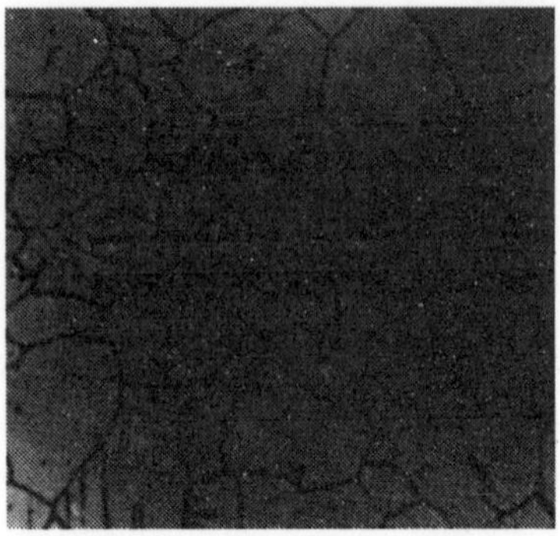

This type of corrosion occurs when a concentration cell is set up because of concentration of electrolyte in contact with metal being non-homogeneous. Due to this corrosion crevices formed on metal surface.

viii. Fretting Corrosion

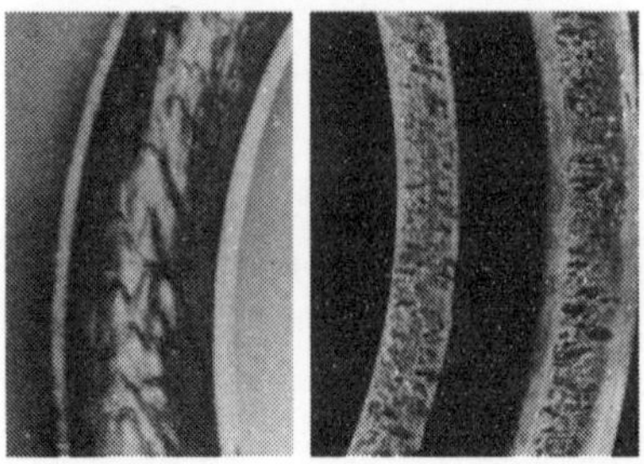

It is defined as the damage occurring at the interface of two surfaces in contact, with each other one or both of which are metals, due to slight relative slip.

ix. Differential Aeration Corrosion:

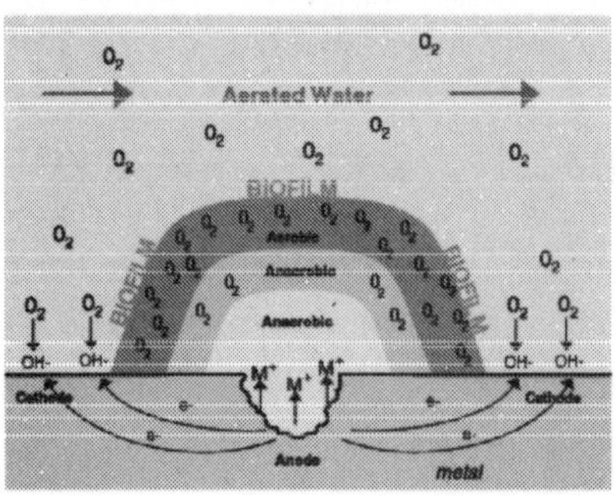

This type of corrosion occurs due to the set up of an oxygen concentration cell resulting from a potential difference caused by different amounts of dissolved oxygen at two locations. Necking in a artifact partly covered by wood is an example of this.

x. Selective Corrosion

In this type of corrosion a solid phase corrode in preference to another solid phase resulting in the selective removal of one component with the help of the corrosion medium. Examples are the destannification in bronzes dezincification in brasses, the graphitization in cast irons

xi. Dew Point Corrosion

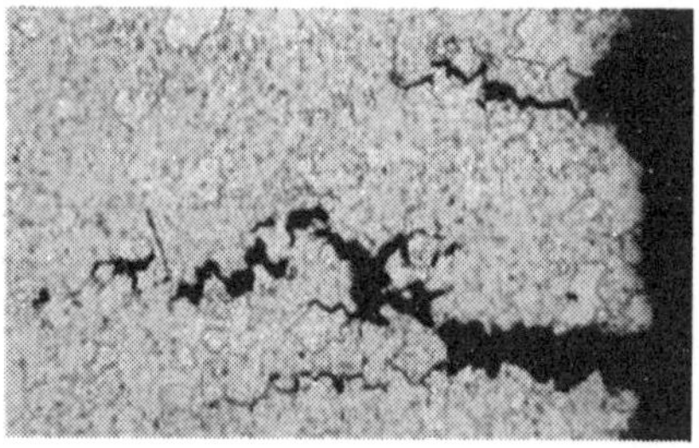

It is a special type of corrosion in which in respect the intermediate between electrochemical corrosion and high temperature oxidation is dew point corrosion. When hot gas in the case of combustion product, are cooled to the condensation point then this type of corrosion occurs. When sulphure dioxide and sulphure tri oxide reach at the its high temperature at 150-200°C then acid form this case and condense are highly corrosive to the iron.

xii. Biological Corrosion

This type of corrosion is caused by the metabolic activity of certain types of microorganisms either directly or indirectly. Micro- organisms can produce a corrosive environment, alter the resistance of the surface film, alter the environment composition, create electrolytic concentration cells on the metal surface or affect the rate of anodic or cathodic reactions.

xiii. Rusting and Atmospheric Corrosion

Upon exposure to the atmosphere the corrosion of iron takes place with formation of rust on the surface in the form of chemical formula $(OH).nH_2O$. Which containing trivalent iron. Iron dissolve as Fe^{++} ions in the anodic reaction and hydroxyl ion s are formed at cathodic site.

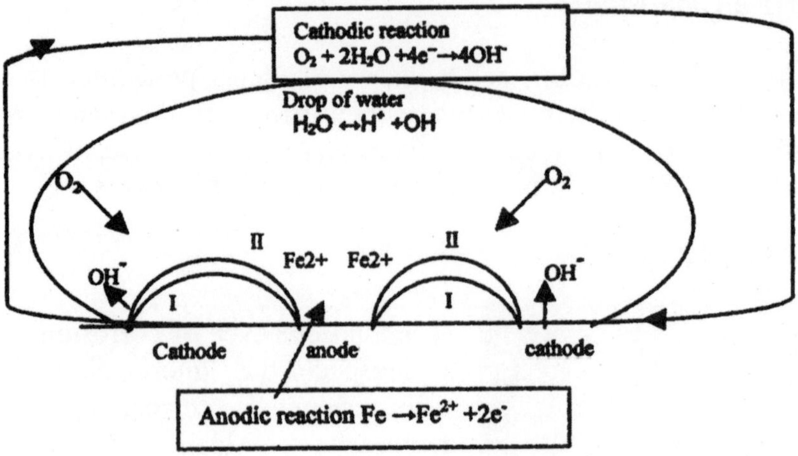

The formation of rust in a drop of water on the surface of iron

The total composition of the atmosphere strongly influences corrosion behavior. The factors like direction of prevailing wind, temperature, rainfall and suspended solid play important role.(P.J Gelling 1985)

11. Factors Responsible for Corrosion of iron artifacts

Corrosion of iron artifacts by dissolved oxygen, water velocity, temperature, organic matter such as marine organisms and other conditions prevailing at the sites where the artifcts are located (Rogers Howard.T 1968:1-46,117-137,272,281)

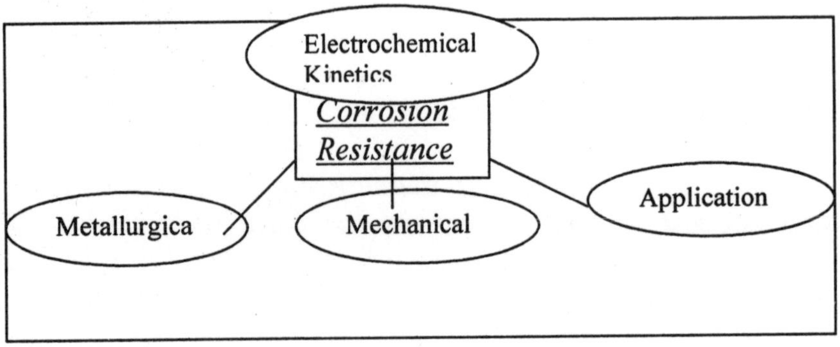

Factors inflecting the corrosion resistance of metal

The highest rate of corrosion in seawater occurs, under conditions of alternate immersion and exposure to the atmosphere, e.g. at splash zones (Von Fraun Hofer J.A 1974) .We are discussing the main factors which are responsible to deteriorate and corrode the iron artifacts underground, marine, open and closed environment.

a. Oxygen

Oxygen is found in dissolved state in seawater or under water due to diffusion from air at the air/ water interface and by metabolic activities (photosynthesis) of marine plants. Oxygen reduction is the principal cathodic reaction in metal corrosion and, therefore, its availability affects the rate of corrosion.

b. pH. (Prudential Hydrogen)

pH of water or an electrolytes play an important role in corrosion of iron artifacts. Changes in pH affect the type, mechanisms and rate of reactions occurring at the anodic and cathodic sites.

c. Temperature

For every $10^{\circ}C$ rise in temperature, the rate of corrosion is expected to be doubled. But the effect of temperature on corrosion is complex as it affects the biological growth rate also.

d. Salinity

In the case of marine environment salinity is the most important factor in reference to corrosion of metal. Salinity affects corrosion rate as it provides a good electrolyte. It forms protective layers on surface of some metal surfaces. It also supplies ions, which catalyze corrosion reactions, and finally it affects the solubility of oxygen in seawater.

e. Water movement

The water movement affects the corrosion rates through metal erosion, destruction of protective films or indirectly by changing the rate of oxygen supply for the cathodic reactions.

f. Presence of other metallic objects (Galvanic coupling)

The presence of other type of metals, nearby, on the site affects corrosion of the object. If the object has lower electrode potential, than the coupling metal, then it corrodes preferentially and at a faster rate, while in case of it having a higher electrode potential than the coupling metal, it will acquire galvanic protection.

g. Marine growths

The marine growths protect the iron artifacts from erosion, mechanical abrasion and other physical damages. They form a microenvironment around the iron artifact due to which the pH at the metal surface is lowered. Which makes barrier to inhibits of corrosion rate of iron artifacts.

h. Sulphate-reducing bacteria

In anaerobic conditions these bacteria contribute largely to the corrosion of metals. They stimulate the cathodic reactions and accelerate the rate of corrosion by secreting the enzymes.

12. Corrosion Mechanism and their Processes

The iron artifacts generally consist of wrought and cast iron. The rates of corrosion of both wrought and cast iron are approximately 0.1mm/ year (North N. A. and Macleod I.D. 1988) . The corrosion of iron in the case of seawater environment is initially with very high rate, often about 0.13 mm/ year, but this rate decreases to a steady and much lower value after sometime.

Cast iron having higher carbon content corroded different manner from wrought iron. The corrosion product of cast iron having carbon content, leaving an intact residue of graphite, which forms a three-dimensional network inside the corrosion product layer, holding the corrosion products together and thus retaining the original shape of the artifacts. The solid phases of cast iron exhibit different susceptibility to corrosion, which increases with decrease in the carbon content of the phases.

Partially corroded cast iron has only graphite remaining on the original surface layer. Needles of cementite are found closer to the residual metal, while areas of pearlite to be deeper into the corrosion product layer and just near the residual metal surface, areas with partially corroded ferrite are located (North N. A. and Macleod I.D.1988:68-98).

In case of wrought iron due to the absence of any graphite layer the original surface of the artifact is not retained in the corrosion products layer. Corrosion follows the same chemical pattern as in cast iron.

In wrought iron salt water penetrates deep into the metal bulk through its slag inclusions causing corrosion along the walls of the slag inclusions, widening them and finally pushing out the slag. This results in cracks formation on the residual metal, giving the metal surface a wood grain appearance characteristic to wrought iron. The corrosion products are soft and have an appearance between delicate separate fibbers and a watery sludge, which easily comes off from the residual metal surface. In the case of water immerged iron artifacts the life history can be divided into four stages on the basis of the changes they undergo as (North N.A. 1982) :

- Initial immersion.
- Concretion with residual metal.
- Concretion with no residual metal.
- Post-excavation.

The period, extending from when the iron artifacts are first submerged into the sea, to when the surface of the artifact is completely covered by concretions is known as initial immersion. During initial immersion, the corrosion behaviour of iron is similar to that of bare iron exposed to water.

The anodic reaction is,

$$Fe \rightarrow Fe^{++} + e^{-}$$

The ferrous ions are oxidized to ferric ions, which precipitate on the metal surface where the pH is about 7.2 to 8.2 . This variable pH is in the case of sea water but it will be varies in the case of under ground soil environment.

$$Fe^{++} \rightarrow Fe^{+++} + e^{-}$$

The cathodic reaction is oxygen reduction and formation of hydroxyl ions at the cathodic sites. It can be represented as:

$$O_2 + 2H_2O \rightarrow 4OH^{-}$$

The compounds observed in the corrosion products layer of iron at this stage are ferric oxy hydroxide, ferrous oxide and amorphous ferric oxyhydroxide.

Fouling organisms, which grow abundantly on iron, as it is nontoxic, forms the concretions covering the artifact surface. They are layers of skeletal materials in the form of calcium carbonate deposited by these marine organisms between these layers, are trapped coral fragments and other debris. Due to low porosity of the concretions exchange of dissolved species between metal surface and the surrounding external water is retarded, resulting in the formation of a microenvironment beneath the concretions.

The remaining dissolved oxygen in the entrapped water in contact with the metal surface is quickly consumed in the cathodic reaction, resulting in the formation of some oxides and hydroxides of iron in the corrosion products. The anodic reaction is;

$$Fe \rightarrow Fe^{++} + 2e^{-}$$

In the microenvironment, the iron ions formed in anodic reaction are hydrolyzed by water forming hydrogen ions.

$$Fe + 2\ H_2O \rightarrow Fe(OH)_2^{\ -} + 2H^+$$

This brings about decrease in pH, at the metal surface, to about 4.8

All over the metal surface acid region are occur during the cathodic reaction which produce hydroxyl ions must be within the concretion layer this reaction may be represent as

$$O_2 + 2H_2O + 4e^- \rightarrow 4OH^-$$

or

$$2H_2O + 2e^- \rightarrow H_2 + 2OH^-$$

At this acidic pH, iron ions become soluble. Some of the previously precipitated iron ions dissolve, forming an acidic solution which contains ferrous, ferric and hydrogen ions and has a pH of about 4.8.

To maintain the charge neutrality the iron-rich acid solution diffuses outward while anions in the form of chloride ions being predominant and most readily available in the immediate surrounding diffuse inwards. This causes the occurrence of high quantity of chloride ions both in corrosion products and concretions.

The iron-rich acidic solution diffuses first through the corrosion products layer, scavenging most of the acid soluble impurities like sulphides, phosphides, alkali and alkaline earth metals. When it reaches to that part of the concretion which is in contact with the corrosion layer ferrous ions displace the calcium ions from the calcium carbonate of the concretions, forming ferrous carbonate. The hydrogen ions dissolve some of the calcium carbonate of concretion forming calcium bicarbonate which causes the pH of the acidic solution to rise resulting in the precipitation of ferrous and ferric ions as oxides, hydroxides and hydroxy chlorides which fill the pores and spaces in the concretion (North N. A. and Macleod I.D. 1988; 68-98) . They also act as cementing materials replacing the original calcite matrix which is slowly dissolving.

The displaced calcium ions come out of the concretion layer and as soon as they come into contact with water pH =8.2 and they re-precipitate as inorganic calcite on the concretion surface. The cathodic reaction in this micro-environment is the evolution of hydrogen in presence of sulphate-reducing bacteria, i.e. in anaerobic conditions

$$2H^{+} + 2e^{-} \rightarrow H_2$$
$$2Fe + S^{--} \rightarrow 2Fe + S$$
$$Fe + S^{--}\ S \rightarrow FeS$$

Iron combines with the sulphide ions to form elemental sulphur and ferrous sulphide. These sulphide ions are produced by the activity of sulphatre-reducing bacteria in the concretions .Ferrous sulphide as the principal compound in the corrosion products in marine iron and the concretions are formed in burial conditions. In concretions of the burial and seabed ferric oxyhydroxide is also significantly present in iron corrosion products. The main oxides in iron corrosion products in burials conditions is ferrous oxide while ferric and ferric hydroxide are the main oxides and hydroxide in exposed conditions. The life history of iron artifacts is characterized by a void inside the concretion in case of wrought iron and complete graphitization in case of cast iron artifacts. Complete corrosion of that metal has occurred , and the artifact is found to be in equilibrium with the surrounding environment (North N. A. and Macleod I.D.1988:68-98).

The next stage corresponds to the changes which the residual metal core and the corrosion products undergo after excavation. This is considered to be a disturbed stage.

The solid present in the corrosion products layer of excavated iron artifacts are those which are thermodynamically stable, under burial condition are geothite and magnetite (Turgoose S -Clarke, R.W. and Blackshaw S.M. 1980:1-7). Chlorides are found in the pores of these solids in the form of a "ferrous chloride" solution.

Upon exposure to atmosphere, oxygen and moisture, after excavation, the ferrous ions are oxidized to akaganeite (FeOOH) in the presence of chloride ions.

$$4\,Fe + O_2 + 6H_2O \rightarrow 4\,FeOOH + 8H^{+}$$

If this reaction occurs away from the metal surface i.e. in the oxide layers of the corrosion products, then the hydrogen ions produced decrease the pH of that locality. The oxides in that region dissolve, resulting in the formation of cracks in the corrosion products layer. Ferrous ions go into solution and together with FeOOH , ferrous ions and hydrogen ions, diffuse out through these cracks and give rise to sweating "beads" on the surface of the deteriorating artifacts. These beads or droplets are highly acidic and contain a large amount of chlorides. They are yellow to brown in colour.

Many iron artifacts have been found to be breaking. When exposed to the atmosphere after excavation. This is due to the combined effects of the precipitation of solid ganeite (FeOOH) from ferrous ions. The volume of iron increases as it passes from ions (Fe ions) to bulkier oxide (FeOOH). This increase in volume in the corrosion products generates stresses inside the artifacts. Secondly the creaks caused by the dissolution of magnetite and other iron oxides by the acidic solution decrease the mechanical strength of the corrosion products layer.

Marine cast iron, after excavation, in presence of atmospheric oxygen and moisture undergoes rapid corrosion where the volume of iron increases from ferrous ions to iron oxide (FeOOH). This exerts a pressure within the graphitized zone leading it to crack and spell off the underlying metal core.

If cracking and spall off do not occur, then the bone between the corrosion layer and residual metal is weakened and corrosion layer may spall off during conservation. Wrought iron is not susceptible to post excavation deterioration as in cast iron as it does not contain graphite or finely divided cementite in its corrosion products. However, it has high chloride contents and if not stored properly or conserved correctly, corrosion of the residual metal will occur and more rapidly than in normal iron. These altered corrosion products are very important in choosing the right conservation methods for marine iron artifacts.

13. Corrosion products of Iron

1. Ferrous Chloride $FeCl_2$

It is found within the pores of the solid corrosion compound in the corrosion products layer (Turgoose S -Clarke, R.W. and Blackshaw S.M. 1980 :1-7). It is present in high concentrations in the yellow beads of liquids in sweating of iron objects (North N.A.1982:75-81) . It is also formed at the metal surface during corrosion of iron in marine environment. It has been identified in corrosion pits where acidic conditions prevail.

2. Ferric Chloride $FeCl_3$

Anhydrous ferric chloride is a covalent compound that dissolves in organic solvents as well as in water. It forms bright-yellow crystals as the hexahydrate. It is found in small quantity in the yellow beads of liquids in seating of iron artifacts together with FeOOH and $FeCl_3$ and hydrogen ions. Ferric chloride is formed during atmospheric oxidation of iron after excavation (Turgoose S -Clarke, R.W. and Blackshaw S.M.1980 :1-7 andNorth N.A.1982:75-83).

3. Ferric oxychloride, FeOCl

It is the major chlorine containing compound of the iron corrosion products (North N.A. and Pearson C. 1977:146-157). It was first reported by PEEV et al in 1978 but later attempts to confirm its presence in marine iron objects is very doubtful as it is very unstable in the presence of water (North N.A.1982:75-83 and Seeley, N.J. and Gilberg, M.R 1981: 50-56).

4. Basic ferrous chlorides

The basic ferrous chloride gets rapid oxidation under normal atmospheric conditions. These chlorides are stable under reducing condition. The three main basic ferrous chlorides are existing as:

Fe (OH) FeCl chloride content 33% by weight.
Fe (OH) FeCl chloride content 23% by weight.
Fe (OH) FeCl chloride content 18% by weight.

As basic ferrous chlorides are formed by precipitation from iron chloride solution, their occurrence in marine iron corrosion products is quite feasible . They undergo rapid oxidation under normal atmospheric conditions to green rust and FeOOH. They are stable under reducing conditions as those found at the metal surface, in corroding marine iron.

5. Ferrous sulphide (FeS_2) or Iron pyrite

It is formed under anaerobic conditions in presence of sulphate-reducing bacteria and it is the major corrosion product of iron artifacts buried in the sediments.

6. Geothite: (FeOOH) or Ferric Oxyhydroxide

It is the most stable corrosion product found in iron. It is formed from practically all corrosion products which are unstable at pH $\leq$ 3.5. It is one of the major solids, 30 to 40%, in corrosion products layer of marine iron (Turgoose S ; 1980: 1-7).

7. Akageneitite: (FeOOH) or - Ferric oxyhydroxide

It is suggested that it is not an original iron corrosion product but formed when object is exposed to dry atmosphere after excavation (Seeley, N.J. and Gilberg, M.R ;1981:50-56).

8. Lepidocrocite :(FeOOH) or Ferric oxyhydroxide.

It is rarely found as iron corrosion product in environment. It is formed under relative oxidizing conditions and an alteration product by following the exposure to atmosphere. The maximum chloride content in this corrosion product can be around 8% by weight. It promotes the rate of corrosion in atmospheric condition.

9. Green rust: Fe(OH)FeOCl

It was first reported by Uyeda and Yoshioka (1946) iron explore from seawater. It is in meta stable and is oxidized to Fe(OH)and FeOCl. There is the chloride content from 7.5 to 8.0 % by weight and this compound associated with higher chloride content compound. It is form between metal and outer oxide layer of Fe^{3+} compounds from the basic ferrous chlorides.

10. Ferric hydroxide $Fe(OH)_3$

It is formed from basic Ferrous Chlorides. By loss of water it is converted to FeO through (FeOOH) Geothite intermediate.

11. Haematite Fe_2O_3 n H_2O, Ferric oxide.

It is red brown in colour and formed from goethite on drying.

12. Magnetite: Fe_2O_3

It is black in colour. It is one of the main components of iron corrosion products together with goethite. Also main corrosion products in buried iron when exposed to atmosphere.

Table 1

Corrosion products	Formula	Mineral
1. Ferric Chloride	$FeCl_3$	Mylosite
2. Ferrous chloride	$FeCl_2$	Lawarencite
3. Ferrous Oxychloride	FeOCl	
4. Basic ferrous chlorides	Fe (OH) FeCl	
5. Ferric Oxyhydroxides	FeO(OH)	Goethite
6. Amorphous Ferric oxyhydroxide	FeO OH	
7. Green-rust	Fe(OH). FeOCl	
8. Ferric oxide	Fe_2O_3	Haematite
9. Ferric oxide	Fe_2O_3 n H_2O FeO	Magnetite
10. Ferrous oxide	FeO	
11. Hydrated Oxide	Fe_2O_3 3 H_2O FeO	Limonite,
12. Ferric Hydroxide	$Fe(OH)_3$	
13. Ferrous sulfide	FeS_2	Iron Pyrite
14. Ferrous carbonate	$FeCO_3$	Siderite

Summarization

The corrosion processes of iron in aquatic environments are generally known but the reactions are too complex and many unpredictable variables are responsible for those reactions. The most of the resulting corrosion products, however, are predictable with a considerable degree of accuracy. This knowledge, while not replacing analytical tests for validation on particular artifact, is usually sufficient to determine what conservation alternatives are required for any artifact if its history is known. The most commonly expected iron corrosion products are:

Sl.	Name of Corrosion Product	Chemical formula	Sl	Name of Corrosion Product	Chemical formula
1.	Ferro-hydroxide	$FeO(OH)$	7.	Ferro-ferrous oxide (black magnetite)	Fe_3O_4 or $FeO{\cdot}Fe_2O_3$
2.	Ferrous hydroxide	$Fe(OH)_2$	8.	Ferric oxide(red brown rust)	$Fe_2O_3.H_2O$
3.	Ferrous chloride, anhydrous	$Fe\ Cl_2$ very damaging	9.	Green hydrated magnetite	$Fe_3O_4.\ H_2O$
4.	Hydrated Ferrous chloride	$FeCl_2{\cdot}xH_2O$	10	Ferric hydroxide (common rust)	$2Fe_2O_3{\cdot}3H_2O$
5.	Ferrous sulphid	FeS	11.	Ferric oxide	Fe_2O_3
6.	Anhydrous Ferric chloride	$FeCl_3$	12.	Hydrated Ferric chloride,	$FeCl_3.H_2O$
			13.	Green rust	$Fe(OH)FeOCl$

The most prevalent iron artifact's corrosion products are ferrous sulphide, magnetite, ferrous hydroxide and iron's chlorides. Many iron artifacts are completely converted to ferrous sulphide, leaving only a loose slush within a natural mold of encrustation. Others completely mineralize to a massive oxide, magnetite, but retain their structural integrity and surface detail but degraded to a loose granular oxide. Iron sulphides are present in varying degrees in each case. Iron chlorides are always a component part of any of the iron corrosion products. The main difference between exposed and buried iron concretions are the prevalence of Fe_3O_4 in buried encrustations and the prevalence of $FeO(OH)$ and Fe_2O_3 in encrustations (North and MacLeod 1987:78).It is especially in high energy zones, such as reefs. Once iron has been removed from its present environment the corrosion process will continue and even accelerated unless certain precautions are taken. It is essential that the artifacts should be properly stored in an inhibitive solution to prevent further corrosion. If the iron in an encrustation is exposed to the air or an uninhibited solution, the ferrous compounds can oxidize to a ferric state which occupies a greater volume on the surface. In this process oxidation of artifact can disfigure a piece and eventually destroy . It is much better to conserve iron artifacts with ferrous corrosion products than iron with ferric corrosion products. Every precaution should be taken to prevent the ferrous corrosion products from oxidizing to ferric products through proper storage and treatment. The greatest damage are possible after recovered from archaeological site due to caused by the iron chlorides. The formation of ferrous chloride can be shown by following reaction:

$$Fe^{+2} + 2Cl^{-} \rightarrow FeCl_2$$

Ferrous chloride oxidizes and turn into ferric chloride and ferric oxide

$$6FeCl_2 + 3O_2 \rightarrow 2FeCl_3 + 2Fe_2O_3$$

Both of the above reactions are gross over simplifications, but the reaction proposed by Eriksen and Thegel (1966;90):

$$Fe + 2NaCl + 2H_2O \rightarrow FeCl_2 + 2NaOH + H_2$$

It is not thermodynamically feasible. Regardless of the exact equation, both the ferrous chloride and ferric chloride combine with water to form hydrates:

$$FeCl_2 + x\ H_2O \rightarrow FeCl_2\,.xH_2O$$

$FeCl_2\,.xH_2O$, and $FeCl_3.\ xH_2O$, where x is normally 2, 4 or 6

These hydrated chlorides causes the trouble to iron artifacts. On exposure to moisture and oxygen they hydrolyze to form ferric oxide or ferric hydroxide and hydrochloric acid. The hydrochloric acid oxidizes to the un-corroded metal to ferrous chloride and hydrogen, or ferric chloride and water. In a simplified form, some or all of the following reactions may continue until no metal remains:

$$Fe - 2e^{-} \rightarrow Fe^{+2}$$
$$Fe^{+2} + 2Cl^{-} \rightarrow FeCl_2$$
$$4FeCl_2 + 4H_2O + O_2 \rightarrow 2Fe_2O_3 + 8HCl$$
$$4FeCl_2 + 7H_2O + O_2 \rightarrow 2Fe_2O_3 \cdot 3H_2O + 8HCl$$
$$2FeCl_3 + 3H_2O \rightarrow Fe_2O_3 + 6HCl$$
$$4FeCl_3 + 9H_2O \rightarrow 2Fe_2O_3 \cdot 3H_2O + 12HCl$$
$$FeO + 2HCl \rightarrow FeCl_2 + H_2$$
$$4FeO + 3O_2 + 12HCl \rightarrow 4FeCl_3 + 6H_2O$$

It is possible by electrolytic reduction to reduce the ferrous compounds like $Fe(OH)_2$, $FeCl_2$, FeS and the ferrous oxide portion of Fe_3O_4, which exists as FeO and Fe_2O_3 . It is not possible to reduce the ferric compounds in an aqueous solution.

The hydrogen sulphide that forms as a metabolic by-product of the bacteria reacts with the metal and accelerates the corrosion process, forming various metal sulphides. This corrosion reaction is most evident on iron if direct contact with wood (North N. A. and Macleod I.D. 1988:68-98).

CHAPTER-FOUR

CONSERVATION

Conservation of Ferrous Artifacts: An Introduction

The various conservation research laboratories around the world are working on developing the new methods and principles for the conservation of archaeological iron artifacts. The outcome and information of these research works are being continuously added to this new discipline, ultimately resulting in methods quickly becoming outdated and changed. Even that all conservation methods have certain drawbacks.

The conservation of archaeological iron being a new field of scientific research and application is still in its infancy. Studies and investigations in the field of archaeological iron conservation are being carried out in many research centers and laboratories in various parts of the world. As a result of research a number of new information are being added to the existing ones bringing about the very fast development of this field. So many of the papers have been published in The Studies in Conservation review, a high level conservation journal in the field of conservation , and in other leading conservation journals.

During the initial development period of scientific study of iron, there were many questions but some are still un-answered, I think archaeological iron artifacts conservation is now experiencing the same stage. Great efforts are being deployed in order to come out with suitable answer to these questions but some are still waiting for answer. The more suitable example is that there is no suitable explanations for certain observations for the similar artifact lying side by side in the same archaeological site and environment have corroded differently.

Some studies have been carried out using idealized conditions which are far from resembling the archaeological site conditions. For understanding clearly the mechanisms involved in corrosion of iron artifacts at the sites, studies should be carried out in situ and with proper materials.

The main cause of accelerated deterioration and corrosion of iron artifacts excavated from the sea and under ground burial sites is the presence of large amounts of chlorides. So for the determination of the correct methods of conservation to be adopted for an artifact, the degree of corrosion, porosity of corrosion layers, chloride distribution, nature of chloride, exact amount of chloride and environmental nature of chloride should be known.

There are different views as to which compound contains the bulk of chlorides in marine iron and burial condition in iron artifacts. Iron chloride first observed and then iron oxichloride in the bulk was suggested by some researchers. Recently, it was suggested that bulk of chloride ions in archaeological iron to be present as compounds like iron oxychloride where the chlorides are adsorbed on the crystal lattice and in the form of solution in the pores of solid corrosion products layer. Another view is that the bulk of chlorides exist as a ferrous and ferric chloride compound.

Identification of the chloride containing compound in archaeological iron artifact is very important because it will definitely help in the development of a more efficient method for chloride removal than the existing ones which are totally or partially unsatisfactory in their theory of action, mode of application and the results they produce.

Inhibitive methods in which use of inhibitors at present though seem to be attractive in theory but it has not been found so successful in practice. Many methods have been used for non-marine iron artifacts conservation, are not applicable in the case of marine iron artifacts. The presently available methods for conservation of marine iron artifacts are coming out- dated and changed in a very short lapse of time. When individual method used for conservation to artifacts do not give satisfactory result, but combination of methods when used has given good and encouraging results.

For the marine and burial archeological iron artifacts, alkaline-sulphite reduction method seems to be the most efficient and successful amongst the washing methods. But for fragile artifacts heat treatment in reducing atmosphere i.e. hydrogen plus nitrogen, is better. Warm heating at 400 °C in hydrogen furnace followed by simple washing also appears to be promising.

The way to tackle the problems in iron artifacts conservation seems to be the adoption of combined methods for removal of the deleterious chlorides, to a certain safe and acceptable level, stabilization by tannin methods in case of cast iron artifacts, followed by microcrystalline wax for surface coating. The iron artifacts after being fully stabilized can be stored or displayed carefully in the controlled environment. The environment should be dry with low relative humidity. If artifacts are displayed in showcases then building up of a microclimate with RH less than 35% would be most desirable for these artifacts.

Observation and periodic checking of artifacts is necessary and if a sign of deterioration becomes visible, then artifacts should be immediately treated for removal of chlorides. The choice of methods lies of course, with the conservator and will be depending upon the state of the corroded artifacts, the quantity and size of artifacts and the time factor.

1. Preliminary Evaluation of Excavated Artifacts on site in respect to Conservation Perspective

Each artifact is removed from an encrustation, it must be carefully partially cleaned, cautiously examined, and its condition evaluated to determine the most appropriate conservation treatment on the excavated site. The artifacts should be classified into one of three categories analogous. The classification are based on weight, size and ratio, close visual inspection, testing the surface with a magnet, probing the corrosion layers with a dental pick, and occasionally using X-rays if facility is available on site.

In the case of the iron artifacts, if it is with a substantial metal core and a consolidated surface capable of withstanding chemical, electrochemical, or electrolytic reduction without any significant changes in the form or dimensions of the artifact. Electrolytic reduction treatment is the preferable in the most cases.

The artifacts that are badly corroded but retain their overall shape, very little or no metal may remain, and there is little overall supporting strength then the treatments would alter the original form. The recommended procedure therefore is to stabilize the artifact by diffusing the soluble chlorides out in an aqueous solution of sodium sesquicarbonate and to consolidate the artifact with a substance such as microcrystalline wax or other suitable synthetic consolidants.

The iron artifacts that are so badly oxidized and fragile then they can only be consolidated. Any further treatment will usually completely disintegrate them. Casting the artifact itself or making a replica from the natural encrustation mold is often the only means of preservation or recovery. Only after these decisions the treatment should be begin.

a. First aid and Preservation of excavated iron artifacts on site

Environment and condition from which true iron artifacts might be retrieved, since iron is so base this will occur only in the presence of phosphate layer or where oxygen is absent. Iron may be preserved either by passivation in deposits of high redox potential and pH due to stiffing by oxide/carbonate crusts or by immunity in deposits of low redox potential that is low concentration of oxygen. Preservation can be prevented by the activity of sulphate reducing bacteria, the presence of chloride ions, or enhanced by phosphates in deposits of low redox potential. An iron artifact from marine sites, in particular, never seems to be found truly well preserved. These artifacts have been observed that they are relatively stable state while on seabed or in burial condition. Once removed from this environment and exposed to the atmosphere they start to deterioration very rapidly and irreversibly, with the result that many artifacts can be totally lost their identities. Therefore it is imperative to take precautionary measures to ensure that the excavated artifacts survive in this critical period between excavation and their delivery to a well equipped conservation laboratory.

Conservation materials with equipments should be at the excavation site before excavation starts unless the artifacts can be transported to the conservation laboratory immediately after excavation.

Artifacts should not be subjected to any adverse conditions that may cause or accelerate their deterioration in the process of photographing, drawing and identification, etc.

Concretions protect to artifact from further damage, so one must be ensure that whether it is absolutely necessary to carry out de-concretion on site, before starting to do so. Before de-concretion, facilities must be available for the subsequent storage, conservation and transportation of the de-concreted artifacts. It is in doubt about the presence and conditions of artifacts inside the concretion, their x-ray radiographs must be done in order to be on safe side if possible otherwise other techniques can be adopted. De-concretion must be done very carefully and in the right manner. No attempt must be made to physical removal of all concretions immediately at one time, otherwise this action damages to artifact. Only readily removable concretions should be physically broken off controlled operations while more adherent ones should be left until metal has been treated and consolidated. De-concretion by mechanical means is easier and safer than chemical methods. The following steps are adopted for the first aid and preservation of archaeological iron artifacts on site.

b. Initial Documentation, Storage and Mechanical cleaning on site

Archaeologists and conservators are equally responsible for conserving the iron artifacts resulting from an archaeological excavation, the basic approach to conservation should be that once an encrustation or any artifact has been delivered to the conservator for the first aid treatment on the site then conservator must adopt first aid conservation process after following steps:

i. Deep Examination of artifacts
ii. Preserve and stabilize the artifact as well as possible,
iii. Recover and collect the useful archeological information.
iv. Acquire accurate and proper data for conservation research.

These type of information are possible only if extensive records are maintained, including detailed descriptions of the artifacts , radiographs if possible , black and white photographs, colour slides, video recording of the procedure adopted during the operation and notes on the preservation procedures utilized.

In the proper records may be include all archaeological data, identifications, descriptions, and the complete conservation procedures of each artifact. The conservation data records, the treatment history of every artifact, thereby accumulating valuable research records on the evaluation of particular conservation techniques.

c. Preliminary cleaning on the excavated sites

Preliminary cleaning should be done with concentration and care. The carelessness damage to the artifacts. Firstly loose mud may be removed with a stream of water or a jet from a plastic bottle with care. Surface wetting agent such as "synperonic NDB" may help to loosen the adherent mud but precaution should be taken to wash all traces of detergent afterwards (Pearson C ;1988:105—116and Robinson W.S ;1981). Care must be taken not to dislodge any surface layers even if sound metal is present beneath while cleaning, as this layer may contain the only surviving evidence of surviving plating and inlays. It is suggested that in case of iron artifacts cleaning can be done by rinsing in tap water or distilled water and the artifacts should always be kept wet condition (Robinson W.S 1981).

If artifact is not possible immediately transported to a laboratory then they should be properly stored onsite. Artifacts should be stored for as short a time as possible as they can deteriorate during storage if correct storage environment is not provided. Leigh recommends 2 to 3 years as the maximum storage period for any archaeological iron artifacts and during this period proper storage conditions are necessary (Pearson C; 1988:105-116)

There are separate methods of de-concretion for the cast iron and wrought iron artifact. Until shown by radiography or a strong pull on a magnet that concretions covering of even small wrought iron artifacts then cleaning is to be taken in another way not like cast iron. Where concretion is solid, as is generally the case of larger iron artifacts, concretion is removed from the artifact before storage otherwise stabilization is difficult to achieve. The soft corroded surface of the artifacts may contain much important information about a archaeological site and its history which would only be obtained if such iron artifacts are cleaned. Selective cleaning may thus seem to be necessary, although such action would bring about the ultimate destruction of the cleaned artifacts.

Chemical and electrolytic techniques are not applicable on site and so manual mechanical methods can be used with small tools or, more commonly; air abrasive with continuous visual examination can be used. Iron artifacts with only a thin layer of corrosion products overlying metal is rare in archaeology but common in historic and ethnographic materials. It would be possible to strip such artifacts by dissolving the iron oxides. This could be achieved with acids but since iron is a base metal, it too will dissolve in many acids and so become etched. Commercial rust removers are usually based on mild inhibited organic acids or phosphoric acids, but they often leave a layer of visible protective deposit over the metal.

Electrolytic cleaning does not have these drawbacks since the iron is catholically protected by electric current from etching and no deposits form. However, all these methods ruthlessly expose existing pits in the metal surface, which is unsightly, and cause plating and inlays to react or become displaced. Due to these dangers, archaeological iron artifacts even of this type is never stripped so abrasive mechanical methods are preferred.

Preserving solution

The artifact should be stored in a corrosion inhibiting solution immediately after excavation and not allowed to dry. A few hours of exposure to the atmosphere may be sufficient to accelerate the deterioration process and creating a parting line between the residual metal core and the graphitized zone. In addition to this, new products are formed which expand in volume forcing off the surface layers. As a consequence of these changes cracks appear in the surface layer and the artifacts may be ultimately disintegrated. This process may take only a few days in many cases.

Iron artifacts can be stored in a 5% w/w solution of sodium carbonate, 2% w/w sodium hydroxide or 5% w/w sodium sesquicarbonate in fresh water (Pearson C ;1988 :105-116 and Robinson W.S ;1981). If distilled water is not available then tap water can be used but for a period not more than 6 months. This method is suitable for both large and small artifacts and removal of concretion is not necessary. Storage in these alkaline solutions keeps out oxygen, neutralizes any acidity due to the presence of chloride ions and forms a passivating film on the metal surface, acting as an anodic inhibitor. The storage containers used may be of polythene or mild steel.

For dry storage for small artifacts silica gel is used as a desiccant. The desiccant can be reactivated by drying in an oven for 24 hours at 110°C. It is important to remove concretions from artifacts stored in this way as they will tend to moisture and chlorides.

2. CONSERVATION OF IRON ARTIFACTS IN LABORATORY

2.1 Preserving the Iron Artifacts before Conservation treatment

The excavated and recovered iron artifacts from archaeological site are equally applicable for any kinds of environments. These excavated and recovered artifacts should be in proper storage under proper prevention to check the further deterioration before starting the conservation. If required, there should use preserving solution.

Artifacts excavated and recovered from archaeological site are usually encrusted together and can have a large form of masses. The encrustation can have a variety of materials. In order to prevent further corrosion, disintegration, breakdown or collapse, encrustation materials must be kept wet up to particular scale between recovery and treatment. Therefore, it is necessary to select a proper preserving solution in which iron artifacts can be safely kept and housed. Many iron artifacts may be quite large and proper solutions should be provided for protection from further corrosion. Some of the problems can be eliminated by leaving the encrustation intact. The encrustation forms an excellent protective coating which retards corrosion, prevents the chemical conversion of the corrosion products already present, protects the artifacts from additional deterioration, and preserves until they can be adequately documented. Once processing has begun and the other materials should be removed if other metal artifacts are also present with iron artifacts, individual artifacts can be placed in a suitable and desirable preserving solution pending for further conservation.

It is recommended that iron artifacts recovered from archaeological sites should be stored in an inhibitive aqueous solution. An inhibitive solution is in any solution containing a substance that diminishes or prevents the corrosion of metals placed in it. Alkaline inhibitive solutions or inhibitive solutions containing oxidizing agents are commonly used on the case of iron artifacts.

The most common alkaline inhibitors are sodium hydroxide, sodium carbonate, and sodium sesquicarbonate. Solutions containing these alkalis can prevent the corrosion of iron in oxygenated water as long as they are in concentrations sufficient to maintain a pH which passivates the iron , makes it chemically inactive, by the formation of an oxide film on the metal. If iron is free of chloride then it can be passivated in a solution with above a pH < 8 (Hamilton 1976:21-25). The rate of deterioration will increase when presence of oxygen and below a pH > 8. In this case the corrosion will be localized and the attack will be even more intense than if no inhibitor had been used (Evans 1963:151). Passivation of iron is difficult at pH below 8, relatively easy at above a pH< 8 and very easy between pH =10 and 12 (Pourbaix 1966:312). Iron will corrode by the formation of hypo ferrate in a solution having above pH =13 and free from oxidizing agents. Thus, if iron is stored in an alkaline solution with the pH maintained between 11 and 13, the iron will remain passified and will not corrode.

If chlorides are not in abundant then five percent sodium carbonate (pH =11.5) and 5% sodium sesquicarbonate (pH =9.7) solutions are sufficient for preserving to iron artifacts. These two solutions are not advisable in presence of high chloride concentrations for prolonged preserving storage unless additional alkali is added or the solution is changed often periodically. Since the pH of these solutions is borderline to the corrosion domain therefore they are not recommended for long term preserving to iron artifacts from a marine environment as well as other environment. These solutions can be used only for short term for preserving purposes.

An inhibited solution containing oxidizing agents can be used for long term storage to the iron artifacts but proper disposal of these used chemical is the main problem. Since these types of used chemicals are prohibited for improper disposal. The extra time is required to monitor the preserving to iron in alkaline solutions.

Chromate compounds, such as potassium chromate, potassium dichromate, and sodium chromate are the effective preserving mixtures. These compounds are more reliable than the alkaline inhibitors as long as the concentration and especially the pH are maintained at safe levels. Chromate solutions prevent corrosion by forming a very thin passivating film of ferric oxide and chromic oxide on the metal surface (Pearson 1972:14). This oxidizing solution creates an environment where a much wide range of pH's and electrode potentials of the surface of the metal is in the passivation range of the metal (Pourbaix 1966:74)

In the emphasized way the solution must be alkaline. The natural alkalinity of chromate, pH =9.1 to 9.3, is an important factor in passivating iron. Dichromate is much more acidic (pH > 7) than chromates and will not passivate iron, unless an alkali is added. The addition of alkali, e.g., NaOH, converts dichromates to chromates and establishes the natural pH of chromate. The protection offered by a chromate solution will break down at too low a pH like the alkaline inhibitors. The chromate can stimulate intense localized attack and create pits covered with a membranous blister of iron hydroxide. The iron hydroxide shields the chromate and allows the anodic reaction (Evans 1963:141). It is necessary that the pH should be maintained in a range of 9.0 to 9.5, otherwise the corrosion attack will be worse if no inhibitors were used. As long as there is free hexavalent chrome (Cr^{+6}), however, the concentration of chloride is not a critical factor as they are in alkaline inhibitors (Worth Carlin 1975). Due to these reasons chromate solutions are particularly suited for the storage of iron from chloride-contaminated environments.

Some of the chromate in the solution is reduced and the solution becomes acidic therefore the pH of the chromate solution needs to be regularly checked. When the solution becomes acidic then additional alkali must be added to convert the dichromates to chromate and maintaining the natural pH range of 9.0 to 9.5. The serious disadvantage of chromate solutions are due it's highly toxicity when ingested and inhaled. They are strong irritants and dangerous to fire risk in contact with organic materials.

The mixture of 0.1N solution of potassium dichromate and 0.1N solution of hydroxide to it may be use to preserving the wrought iron. It has been reported that wrought iron artifacts recovered from the archaeological sites have been stored in this solution for more than three years with no apparent corrosion was observed. Sodium hydroxide should not have to be added in the chromate solution unless the solution becomes acidic as the chrome is reduced. Periodically the pH may have to be adjusted and maintained at 9.0 to 9.5 by the addition of sodium hydroxide.

It is also recommend that for the conservation of iron artifacts the preserving solutions should be prepared with distilled or de-ionized water. If the chloride content is less in tap water than chloride content in artifact then solution can be prepared in local tap or well water. In this case there is no advantage to mixing up a solution with expensive distilled or de-ionized water only to have it contaminated with chloride well in excess of the local water supply. Tap water should continue to be used for all preserving solutions and electrolytes until the chloride level is less. Using rain water in electrolytes between tap water and de-ionized water is advisable.

Distilled water is recommended occasionally as a preserving solution for iron artifacts. Unaltered de-ionized or distilled water should never be used. They are generally slightly acidic and hence highly corrosive. Likewise, when used for rinsing or as a bath for detecting chlorides, the duration should be kept to minimum and adequate precautions.

2.2.1 Conservation Procedure for Iron Artifacts

The process by which iron artifact is cleaned is determined by the preliminary evaluation and only then can the appropriate conservation measures be taken. The conservation treatments accorded an artifact of iron will be discussed under the following categories:

A Documentation and Storage
B. Conservation:
   i. Preliminary steps
      1. Mechanical de-concretion
      2. Chemical de-concretion
   ii. Removal of chlorides
      1. Washing methods
      2. Heat treatment methods
      3. Electrochemical cleaning
         a. Galvanic cleaning
         b. Electrolytic reduction cleaning
      4. Chemical cleaning
      5. Annealing
      6. Water diffusion in alkaline solutions
C. Final documentation and storage

2.2.1.1 Documentation and Storage

Conservator is responsible for conserving the iron artifacts come from an archaeological excavation site in the laboratory. The basic approaches for the conservation should be :

- Preserve and stabilize the iron artifacts if required
- Collecting the useful historical and archeological information
- Acquire data for conservation research.
- Prepare a data sheet
- To collect all data in a prescribed data sheet

As possible an extensive records are maintained and all records should be well organized in a filing system so the data will be readily accessible. If any artifact needs re-treatment in the future the card provides important information that why the original treatment was failed and how to reverse the process. Considerable archeological data exists in the form of associations and provenience of artifacts within each encrustation. This information is recoverable only by "in situ" observation and recording by the conservator. In other words, the conservator is in a unique position to supply invaluable archeological data and necessary details of the artifacts. The deterioration of archaeological iron artifacts is mainly brought about by the chloride ions found to be present in both, their corrosion products layer and residual metal cores. These chloride ions accelerate the rate of corrosion reactions to such an extent that the amount of corrosion occurring in a few days will be the same as that the metal will undergo in absence of chloride ions, in months or even years.

In the case of marine and non marine burial iron artifacts, the metal inside the concretion has reached certain stability and in equilibrium state with its immediate surroundings. Upon excavation of the artifact, this equilibrium is disturbed as the artifact is introduced in to a new environment, leading to rapid deterioration of the artifact if it is not properly stored or no proper on site treatments are provided.

The iron artifacts excavated from archaeological sites can be classified as cast iron and wrought iron. Due to difference in carbon content they corrode differently, forming different corrosion products. Thus, there is a difference in the manner in which they are conserved. In the case of cast iron the residual metal together with the graphitized corrosion product should be preserved while in case of wrought iron it is not necessary to preserve the loose corrosion products. The main aim of conservation of iron artifact is the removal of the deleterious chloride ions contained within the corrosion products and the residual metal core. The amount of chloride ions in iron corrosion products is found to very considerably even within the same artifact. The value of chloride contents for iron artifacts from archaeological sites is very high, between 6-12% by weight and it is suggested that the majority of chlorides may be found in some iron and chloride compounds, which must be containing appreciably more than 13% by weight of chlorine (North N.A 1988:207-254) .

Turgoose 1980:1-10 suggested that the chloride ions might be contained in solution in water within the pores of the corrosion products of the archaeological iron. The chlorides trapped within the lattice structure of various iron oxyhydroxides and present in the pockets of hydrated ferrous chlorides at the interface between the metal and the corrosion products layer constitute the bulk of the chlorides in the iron artifacts (Seeley, N.J.and Gilberg, M.R 1986:50-56).There is no general argument and agreement on what level of chloride left in the artifact after treatment will be safe. The safe chloride level seems to be dependent on the environmental conditions where the artifact is to be displayed or kept after treatment. The safe residual chloride level in a humid area will be lower than that of a dry area. In the hot with low humidity environment, it was found that for 100 to 800 ppm of residual chloride level in iron artifacts, yellow droplets of iron chloride appeared on the surface of artifact but spalling of the graphitized layer in cast iron did not occur (North N.A 1988:207-254) .Above of the 800 ppm of residual chloride level, spalling of graphitized layer occurred often several months and years after treatment 100 ppm residual chloride level is accepted as being safe. After removal of chlorides from the corrosion layers and the residual metal core, the accelerated corrosion rate is reduced to the normal rate at which conventional anti- corrosion methods can be operate effectively for the successful stabilization of the iron artifact .

Basically the methods involved in the removal of chlorides from iron artifacts are washing methods where chlorides are extracted from the artifact by immersing it in an appropriate wash solution; chloride release is diffusion controlled, and in heat treatment methods where by heating the artifacts, chlorides are eliminated through their volatilization.

The Conservation of Antiquities and Works of Art (Plenderleith and Werner 1971) have a general references for the conservation of archeological iron artifact in any environment.

Sea-recovered iron artifacts have most difficult problems, but most of the conservation procedures used on them can be applied equally to iron from other archeological environments. The absence of marine encrustation and excessive chloride contamination considerably reduces the length of time required to process and stabilize non marine iron artifacts. If the conservators understand the corrosion and preservation problems of artifacts from a salt water environment and is familiar with the alternative procedures that can be utilized, they can cope with iron artifacts from any other archeological context. Whatever conservation technique(s) is utilized, it is essential to understand that no treatment is sufficient unto itself. It is a part of a series of conservation processes designed to assure that a lasting preservation will be achieved. The duties of conservation laboratories are to take iron artifacts as received and delivered a stabilized artifacts.

2.2.1.2 CONSERVATION PROCESS

A. Preliminary steps

2.2.1.2.1. Mechanical de-concretion

During delivery the iron artifacts to the conservation laboratory, archeological iron artifacts may be typically covered with a dense and often thick encrustation. Removing the artifacts from this tough mass is analogous to iron artifacts from inside concrete blocks. Since most of the artifacts are hidden from their view, radiographs are indispensable for determining the context of an encrustation. It is serving as a guide in extracting the artifacts from the encrustations. In order to x-ray of large encrustation, large industrial x-rays machine such as 260 KVP water cooled Picker Industrial X-ray can be used. Small to medium size encrustations up to approximately 4 x 4 feet can be X-rayed intact and most of the constituent artifacts identified. It is often desirable to make a tracing or overlay from the individual X-ray plates (24" x 24" is an ideal size film). On the overlay all the discernible artifacts are to be traced. If any artifact is not detectable on the radiographs then it can be drawn in and their correct provenience located as they are encountered in the encrustation. Useful notations such as catalogue numbers, condition of artifacts can easily be added to the overlay.

For removing the encrustation, mechanical cleaning is the only feasible alternative. To accomplish this, a variety of hammers and chisels are indispensable, especially on the very large pieces. By hammering and chiseling along cleavage lines, the encrustation can be detached from large artifacts with little or no damage to the artifacts. For the extraction of smaller artifact, however, pneumatic tools are more efficient and less destructive. Chisels are useful to the particularly removing large amounts of encrustation from less fragile artifacts. Smaller and more precisely controlled, Pneumatic air scribes, with their more delicate scribes and various chisels, which can be custom made in the laboratory, are ideal for removing the encrustation from small, fragile pieces and for getting into restricted place of the artifacts. The pneumatic air scribe is much more durable than any comparable electric scribes or vibro- tools. Combined use of the two types of pneumatic tools, the chisel and the scribe, is often necessary. They can be most effective in freeing movable parts.

When in doubt as to how much to mechanically removed, it is much safer to leave a thin layer of encrustation on the surface of the iron artifacts where the original surface can not be determined. When the artifact is placed in electrolysis, the evolution of hydrogen bubble at the surface of the metal will loosen the encrustation and mechanically remove any encrustation left on the metal. While electrolysis can be used to remove encrusted artifacts, the whole process of conservation is considerable speeded up, if the encrustation removal is aided by mechanically removing as much of the encrustation can be do by hand. A suggested procedure is to be used a hammer or chisel to remove as much as possible of the encrustation from the artifacts. Then a sandblaster can be employed to cut through the encrustation. Periodically a steel rod, ground to a chisel-like point, should be used to roughen the surface of the encrustation so that the sand will work more efficiently. This technique may sound brutal, but actually very little, if any, harm can do to artifacts. The sandblaster will actually cut a hole through the encrustation without touching the metal. That is, a layer of encrustation which is usually left on the surface. If necessary, additional encrustation can be removed with iron rods or other tools. Once a hole is made through the artifact, the artifact can be set up in an electrolytic bath with a center auxiliary anode. Hydrogen evolution from the artifact will remove the remaining encrustation. The use of acids is generally a slow, ineffective process. Acids, especially hydrochloric acid , attack the metal oxide as readily as the encrustation and so, are too damaging to metal. Even successful chemical techniques pose problems in recording association, observation, and measurements and in making casts from molds of completely oxidized artifacts.

It has been reported that when encrusted iron artifacts are placed in electrolysis then the encrustation is loosened off the surface. This technique known as "deganquing" (Montlucon 1986; 1987) .It can be quite effective on an encrusted artifacts but can be act as destructive when used on encrustation containing possible molds of corroded artifacts that can be cast in epoxy resin. Some information about encrustations is in the form of associations that must be visually documented by the conservators. "Deganguing" is an effective tool that has been in use in varying degrees for years. But it should be used with carefully when working with complex, heavily encrusted artifacts that may contain other artifacts also.

Hammer, geopicks, and other tools are used for de-concretion of large artifacts. Blows are given perpendicular to the surface of the artifact with the flat end of the hammer. With a series of hits, a small area of the concretion is made to loosen and this is gently praised loose by hand. Blows should not be struck at an angle as this may cause the concretion to tear out and carry with it part of the artifact. Care must be exercised not to hit the exposed surface of the artifact with the hammer (Pearson C 1988:105-116). The concretion protects the artifacts from physical and chemical damage in the course of transportation from the archaeological sites to the conservation laboratory. So it is preferable to carry out de-concretion in this case in the laboratory. During de-concretion, the concretions and artifacts must never be allowed to dry in order to avoid rapid air degradation. A hose playing tap water or seawater in the case of on site conservation, on the artifacts can be used to keep them wet. Cast iron artifacts have a graphitized surface layer which is soft, so de-concretion should be carried out very carefully as it can be readily damaged. This graphitized layer retains metallurgical information and the original shape of earthen artifacts.

The concretions inside a cast iron artifact are to be removed by using a hydraulic drill, with a hollow silicon carbide-tipped lit, having an external diameter fractionally larger than that of the artifact. This method enlarges so its diameter should be recorded before de-concretion. If the diameter of the drill used is smaller than that of the artifact, then graphitized layer is to be affected of large artifact. From one side of the inside of the artifact will be removed. While drilling a artifact may still contain some shots and charge, so progress of drilling must be carefully inspected from time to time to avoid damage of artifact. All the above operation must be completed in controlled way otherwise the artifacts can be affected and possibilities of damage may be increase.

2.2.1.2.2. Chemical De-concretion

The chemical de-concretion of a artifact is a uncontrolled process so that the great care is needed while using acids for removal of concretions and this is preferably done in the laboratory if more urgent are required, not on site. In the case of iron artifacts, the concretions are virtually insoluble except in extreme acidic conditions where the corrosion products on the artifacts will also be affected. It is recommended that first remove the bulk of concretions and then give acid treatments as large quantities of acids are needed to dissolve archaeological concretions (Pearson C 1988:05-116). The final de-concretion must be done chemically or after the consolidation of artifact.

Preliminary cleaning in the laboratory should be done with great care. If loose mud and clay is there then it may be removed with a stream of water or a jet from a plastic bottle with controlled operations. Surface wetting agent such as "synperonic NDB" may help to loosen the adherent mud but more precautionary measure should be taken to wash all traces of detergent afterwards (Pearson C 1988:05-116and Robinson W.S1981). Care must be taken not to dislodge any surface layers even if sound metal is present beneath while cleaning, as this layer may contain the only surviving evidence of surviving plating and inlays also. In case of iron artifacts cleaning is done by rinsing in tap water or distilled water. The artifacts should always be kept wet during the chemical de –concretion (Robinson W.S1981).

REMOVAL OF CHLORIDES

a. Washing Methods

The main intention of washing method is to remove chlorides of the iron artifacts if present in the form of ferrous and ferric compound. The principle behind the washing methods can be represented by the following equation.

$$\underset{\text{solid}}{Fe(OH)Cl} + \underset{\text{wash solution}}{X} \rightarrow \underset{\text{solid}}{Fe(OH)X} + \underset{\text{wash solution}}{Cl^-}$$

Where X may be hydroxides, bicarbonates or carbonates

The hydroxyl ions, first diffuse in the corrosion product, react with the chlorine containing compounds and displace chloride ions as free ions which diffuse out of the corrosion product into the wash solution. The chloride ion diffusion through the corrosion product is the rate controlling step. But when sodium carbonate or sodium bicarbonate is used the chloride ions release is slower because of a decrease in the inward diffusion rate of carbonate and bicarbonate ions. The rate of chloride ions release into wash solution follows the diffusion law.

To improve the rate of chloride release, the conservator can alter only the chloride ion diffusion coefficient 'D'in the corrosion product, which is found to be highly dependent on the porosity of the sample. This means that the diffusion of chloride ions occurs through the solution filled pores and thus the more pore space present in the corrosion products layer, the faster will be the movement of ions. The increase the porosity of the corrosion products layer, it means is to convert the iron compounds found in the corrosion products to a denser state (North N.A 1988). This can be achieved by reduction on the iron compounds.

$$3\ FeOOH + e^- \rightarrow FeO + 2H_2O$$

This reaction produces a volume reduction (i.e. increase in density) of approximately 1.7 cm for every mole of FeOOH reduced (North N.A 1988:207-254). The above reduction can be brought about by

1. Electrolysis
2. Alkaline sulphite reduction and
3. Hydrogen furnace reduction.

The rate of chloride ions release into wash solution follows the diffusion law which is represented as:

$Q \propto (D\ t)$ ½ for initial stages of washing and

$Q \propto (1\text{-}K\exp.(-k\ D\ t/d^2)$ for later stages of washing.

Where Q is the quantity of chloride released.

T is the treatment time.

D is the chloride ion diffusion coefficient in the corrosion product.

K and k are constants dependent on the shape of the artifact.

d is the thickness of the corrosion layer

Large increases in D values, which greatly enhance the rate of an ion outward diffusion through the corrosion product, are obtained with these methods.

The D value in an untreated graphitized cast iron from the marine artifact was found to vary from 1.0 to 10 cm / sec (North N.A 1988: 207 – 254). After reduction the D values were between 5.0×10 to 2.5×10 cm / sec for alkaline sulphite reduction , between 1.0×10 to 8.0×10 cm/sec for electrolytic reduction and between 5.0x10 to 1.0×10 cm/ sec for hydrogen furnace reduction (400°C).The reason for greater increase in D value for hydrogen furnace reduction than in alkaline sulphite and electrolytic reductions .These are methods of the main reaction occurring in the corrosion layer in which the reduction of FeOOH to denser magnetite,

$$3\ FeO(OH) + H^{+} + e^{-} \rightarrow Fe_3O_4 + 2\ H_2O$$

While in the formed method both magnetite and metallic iron are formed

$$3Fe_2O_3 + H_2 \rightarrow 2\ Fe_3O_4 + H_2O$$
$$Fe_3O_4 + 4H_2 \rightarrow 3\ Fe + 4H_2O$$

The chloride ion diffusion rate increase can also be brought about by increasing the mobility of ions in the solution, by alternate heating and cooling of the de-ionized water means washing method and the use of Lithium hydroxide/ Methanol method.

The increase in the rate of chloride diffusion by hot solution method was found to be not only due to the mobility of the chloride ions but mainly due to the conversion of amorphous ferric hydroxide to denser magnetite resulting in the increase in porosity of the corrosion products layer (North N.A. and Pearson C 1978:174-186). However, in this method the increase in porosity, and hence increase in the rate of chloride release, is comparatively lower than in reduction methods.

As for lithium hydroxide/methanol method, theoretically there must be a higher chloride extraction rate due to higher solubility of ferric chloride in methanol as compared to sodium hydroxide method. But in practice lithium hydroxide/methanol method is found to be no more effective than sodium hydroxide method in chloride removal from marine iron artifacts. 0.5M Sodium hydroxide found to be twice as efficient for chloride extraction from archaeological iron as 0.05 M lithium hydroxide/methanol (Watkinson, D Clarks, R.W. and Blackshow S.M 1980:28-80).

i. Sodium Hydroxide method (Simple washing)

The principle involved here can be represented as,

$$\underset{\text{Solid}}{Fe(OH)Cl} + \underset{\text{wash solution}}{NaOH} \rightarrow \underset{\text{Solid}}{Fe(OH)} + \underset{\text{Wash solution}}{OH^- \text{ and } Na^+}$$

In this method of washing simply involve the diffusion law. The iron chloride compounds although insoluble in water but react with hydroxyl ions present in wash solution (North N.A 1988:207-254) . The chloride ions are displaced by hydroxyl ions from the sodium hydroxide and they diffuse out into the wash solution. After mechanical removal of concretions, the artifact is placed in a suitable container and then completely covered by 2% by weight of sodium hydroxide solution in distilled water. The weight of artifact to volume of solution ratio recommended is 1:4 to 1:9 and 1:5 to 1:6 ratio is desirable as volume of the solution is not excessive and that at this ratio natural convection currents within the solution will maintain the necessary concentration gradients (Watkinson, D. Clarks, R.W. and Blackshow S.M 1980:28-40 and North N.A 1988:207-254). So the need for stirring will not arise.

The rate of the chloride release from the artifact is monitored and solution changed as needed. The duration time for immersion is 30 to 40 days with one change of the wash solution at 15 days (Watkinson, D. Clarks, R.W. and Blackshow S.M 1980:28-40). The amount of chloride in the wash solution is normally determined by Mohr titration, Potentiometer titration, mercuric nitrate titration or calorimeter methods.

When the amount of chloride ions in the wash solutions remains constant, the completion of extraction chloride then in order to wash out the sodium hydroxide solution from the artifact, it is immersed for at least 4 weeks in distilled water. Then for at least and other week in distilled water containing 1000 ppm of either sodium nitrite or sodium dichromate which play the role of corrosion inhibitors (North N.A 1988:207-254).

With the first wash in distilled water the amount of sodium hydroxide diffused into the water from the artifact is enough to raise the pH of the wash water to 10 or higher thus inhibiting any iron corrosion. While in the second wash the amount of sodium hydroxide released is much less than the first wash and a separate inhibitor is required to inhibit any corrosion process to set up.

If the amount of sodium hydroxide removed from the artifact is insufficient, then white crystals of sodium bicarbonate will appear on its surface which may lead to cracking of the graphitized zone of cast iron or the lifting of paint layers on wrought iron. For this method complete removal of concretions is desirable as this forms a surface barrier, greatly retarding the release of chlorides from the underlying corrosion product layer.

The pH of the wash solution should be checked monthly as sodium hydroxide absorbs carbon dioxide from the air and is slowly converted to sodium carbonate and sodium bi carbonate resulting in the lowering of the pH of wash solution. This method is easy to carry out, imposes less stress on the artifact and requires a minimum of preparation. This method is not so suitable for stabilization of archaeological iron as all chloride ions are not extracted this leaving the residual metallic core potentially unstable (Watkinson, D. Clarks, R.W. and Blackshow S.M 1980:28-40). If the amount of chloride left in the artifact is 76 ppm or more, then it will nullify any inhibitive effects of sodium carbonate which might be formed by the reaction of carbonate with the residual sodium hydroxide in the artifact. This method does not consolidate or harden the graphitized surface, in cast iron artifact, which remains very susceptible to physical damage.

For heavily corroded iron, this method gives inconsistent results. In general for marine iron artifacts which are corroded to a depth of 3 mm or more, this method alone is not efficient but if the artifact are pretreated such that their porosity is increased, then this method gives consistently successful results.

ii. Sodium Sesquicarbonate Method

In 1912, Scott suggested the use of sodium sesquicarbonate for extraction of chloride ions from iron artifacts. The principle involved here is the same as that of sodium hydroxide method and can be represented by the equation.

$$\underset{\text{solid}}{Fe(OH)Cl} + \underset{\text{wash solution}}{X} \rightarrow \underset{\text{solid}}{Fe(OH)X} + \underset{\text{wash solution}}{Cl^-}$$

X is bicarbonate and carbonate ions.

In this case the chloride release rate is slower in comparison to sodium hydroxide method due to decrease in the inward diffusion rate of x species i.e. bicarbonate and carbonate ions (North N.A 1988:207-254) . In this method, water removes the soluble salts from the corrosion products layer while sodium sesquicarbonate prevents further rusting (Oddy W.A. and Hughes M.J 1970:183-189).The artifacts after removal of concretions are completely immersed in the wash solution in a vessel which is covered with a clock glass or sheet of aluminium foil to prevent contamination and evaporation of the solution. Use of 5% W/V of sodium sesquicarbonate solution in de-ionized water has been recommended ((Oddy W.A. and Hughes M.J 1970:183-189) .The solution is to be changed daily for a week to remove large quantities of chloride which wash out initially. Then wash solution is changed weekly for ten weeks. The presence of chloride in the wash solution is tested by silver nitrate method or any other methods.

The wash solution is now left to stand for four weeks, after which it is tested for presence of chloride ions. If chloride ions level is found to be unchanged, it indicates the completion of washing. In case if chloride ions level rise, then the procedure of weekly washings is repeated until the chloride level becomes stable.

It was found that by heating the solution at 50°C the rate of chloride removal did not increase (Oddy W.A. and Hughes M.J 1970:183-189). But when alternate heating and cooling was effected, due to the expansion and contraction of capillaries in the metal and in the corrosion products layer, increase in the rate of chloride extraction occurred.

iii. Lithium Hydroxide and Methanol Method

Lithium hydroxide method was first suggested by R. Ake-Bresle in 1974. He experimented on modern steel surfaces which were not extensively corroded. The principle behind this method is that the chlorides contents in the artifact react with Lithium hydroxide to form lithium chloride which having a high degree of solubility in alcohols and other organic solvents are drawn into the wash solution.

$$2LiOH + Cl_2 \rightarrow 2\,LiCl + 2OH^-$$
$$FeCl_3 + 3LiOH \rightarrow Fe(OH)_3 + 3LiCl$$

The artifact after de-concretion and cleaning is completely dehydrated in alcohol or a mixture of alcohol by vigorous stirring and repeatedly changing the baths. The dehydration is essential as even a small residue of water may invalidate the whole process. Different solvents and concentrations of lithium hydroxide have been used by different workers. Bresle in 1974 used a concentration of 0.2% lithium hydroxide in methanol, Fabech and Trier in 1978 used 0.2% in a mixture of methanol and isopropanol. North and Pearson in 1978 used a 0.4% methanol while D. Watkinson 1980 used a 0.2% in ethanol.

The artifact is placed in a tightly sealed glass tank and completely covered with a volume, of lithium hydroxide / Methanol, which is six times the weight of the artifact, i.e. a ratio of 1:6. North and Pearson 1978 used a 1:10 days (Watkinson, D. Clarks, R.W. and Blackshow S.M. 1980:28-40). The advantage of this method is that it is much less violent as compared to all other washing methods used in the conservation of iron artifact. It is non aqueous and, therefore, there will be little or no corrosion taking place during treatment. It also requires less attention during treatment.

The drawbacks of this method is that the residual lithium chloride in the corrosion products after treatment, being hygroscopic will form a solution at low relative humidity's in almost any storage environment and thus stimulate further corrosion (Watkinson, D. Clarks, R.W. and Blackshow S.M 1980). But due to the very small quantity of lithium chloride which is carried over from the treatment solution it is unlikely to cause serious problem. This method requires sealed containers since the alcohols are highly in flammable. Krakow in 1978 treated marine iron artifacts by this method were found to corrode only after 8 to 9 months after treatment (Organ R.M 1978) . The chloride extracted by this method, come mainly from compounds like ferric chloride which are highly soluble in lithium hydroxide and alcohol solution (North N.A. and Pearson C 1978:174-186). But the main chloride containing compound in marine iron is a Fe-Cl compound which remains unaffected by lithium hydroxide and alcohol.

In this method could not extract all chlorides from iron artifacts so it is not suitable for removal of chlorides from archaeological iron as it leaves the metallic core in a potentially unstable state. The Lithium carbonates residues remaining on the surface of artifact after treatment and does not impart any inhibitive properties to the artifact (Watkinson, D Clarks, R.W. and Blackshow S.M 1980: 28-40).

In this method a black surface of artifact is not produced so it is considered for iron artifacts which having little corroded surfaces with fragile surface layers. Due to the high activity coefficient of chloride ions in non-aqueous solvents chloride ions may be adsorbed into compounds such as goethite, causing the retention of large amount of chloride ions in the corrosion products (Turgoose S 1982;97-101).

iv. The Alkaline Sulphite Reduction Method

The alkaline sulphite treatment was developed by North and Pearson in1975 to stabilize archaeological cast iron, but is also used on wrought iron. Bryce in 1979 found that the treatment is effective on iron artifacts that are moderately to heavily corroded, but they must have a metallic core. Otherwise, the iron artifact breaks up during treatment. The procedure is as follows:

After mechanically cleaned artifacts immersed in a solution of 0.5 M (20 g/l water) of sodium hydroxide and 0.5 M (126 g/l water) of sodium sulphite. Tap water can be used for this purpose for first one or two baths thereafter de-ionized or distilled water should be used for final bath. The container should be filled as full as possible and sealed to prevent any access to air. Sealing of container is necessary to avoid the conversion ions by atmospheric oxygen, thereby decreasing the reductive capacities of the wash solution .The solution is mixed and the artifact placed in it as quickly as possible to avoid any oxidation of the solution. The container is placed in an oven and kept gently warmed or heated to a temperature of 60-90 °C for a week. During this period the solution may develop a brownish colour. The artifact is then removed from the bath and put into fresh solution. This treatment is repeated for 8 weeks or until no brown colour is seen at the end of the immersion period. After this, two solution changes are effected. The artifact is then removed and treated by simple washing (sodium hydroxide method) until chloride release is minimum or stable. The artifact is then washed with distilled water as in case of simple washing to remove the excess of sodium hydroxide solution

The artifact is processed through several baths until chlorides are eliminated; this may take from a week to several months and numerous baths. The solution does not attack any residual metal so there is no danger of too many baths.

When a archaeological iron artifact is immersed in this hot reducing solution, the iron corrosion compounds are converted to magnetite and the chlorides are transferred to the solution where they are discarded with each bath change. The artifacts come out of the treatment with a very black surface colouration. Since the solution is strongly alkaline, contact with the skin should be avoided.

Once the alkaline sulphite stabilization treatment is completed, the artifacts are washed for one or more hours in several baths of de-ionized water and then placed in a 0.1 M solution of barium hydroxide (32 g. per liter of water). Barium hydroxide is slightly poisonous, so contact with the skin should be avoided. If the artifact is intensely rinsed in several baths of de-ionized water following the alkaline sulphite stabilization, the barium hydroxide baths can be eliminated.

The alkaline treatment is very effective for conserving iron recovered from a marine environment or other environments. The main drawbacks of the treatment are that it has to be carried out in an air tight container and the solution should be kept heated.

The principle of this method involves the reduction of ferric oxychloride and ferric oxyhydroxide (FeOOH) compound of specific gravity. 2.4 to 3.6 g/cm in the corrosion products to the denser magnetite (Fe_3O_4) with specific gravity 5.2 g/cm, thereby increasing the porosity of the corrosion products layer and achieving a more rapid diffusion of the chloride ions into the wash solutions:

$$SO_3^{2-} + 2OH^- \rightarrow SO_4^{--} + H_2O + 2e^-$$
$$3FeOOH + e^- \rightarrow Fe_3O_4 + 2H_2O + OH^-$$

The electron for the reduction of ferric oxyhydroxide FeOOH are supplied by sulphide ions which is converted to sulphite ions (North N.A 1988: 207 – 254) · According to Gilberg and Seeley (1982) the mechanism involved for the reduction of ferric oxyhydroxide FeOOH by sodium sulphite (Na_2SO_3) in presence of hydroxyl ions is different. (Gilberg M.R. and Seeley J.N 1982:180-184) . Alkaline sulphite method is a far more complicated process and magnetite is not formed as a result of the direct reduction of ferric oxyhydroxide by sodium sulphite in the absence of ferrous ions. Ferric chloride can be reduced to magnetite by sodium hydroxide but at high pH ferric chloride first precipitates as amorphous ferric oxyhydroxide via polymerization of ferric hydroxide $Fe(OH)_3$ and this amorphous compound is reduced to magnetite by sodium sulphite

Chloride extraction by this method is highest when the concretions are not allowed to dry in the atmosphere after excavation (Gilberg M.R. and Seeley J.N 1982:180-184). This method will be most effective when carried out on artifacts immediately after their excavations because without the exposure to atmosphere, transformation of ferrous compounds and amorphous materials present, to ferric oxyhydroxides which would not be capable of undergoing reduction to magnetite in absence of ferric ions, will not occur.

The increase in diffusion coefficient in alkaline sulphite reduction may be high when compared to simple washing methods (North N.A 1988:207-254). The graphitized zones of cast iron are hardened and the surface markings are also retained. The colour of the treated artifact surface is dull matt black which is considered to be aesthetically acceptable. This method appears weaken the bond between the corrosion layer and the residual concretion which can be quite easily removed. But it is preferable to remove the bulk of the concretion before treatment. When chloride is present in form of ferrous and ferric chloride, its removal is unsuccessful by this method (Organ R.M 1978). The sulphite ions hinder with the chloride analysis and rendering for inaccurate analysis.

When corrosion layer is thick, more than 15 mm thickness then adequate chloride extraction in a reasonable time is not achieved and also problem in removing the residual reactants is encountered. Barium salts which are used for removal of sulphate ions are not easily removed and form efflorescent unsightly white crystals on the surface of artifact. But they are not harmful to the artifact. Alkaline sulphite reduction method has the practical drawback of requiring high temperatures and sealed containers (Turgoose S 1982:97-101).

The higher chloride extraction efficiency is probably due to, the conversion to the magnetite lattice, structure, rather than the subsequent increase in corrosion product density or, the presence of highly alkaline solutions (Seeley, N.J. and Gilberg, M.R 1981:50-56). It appears that the greater effectiveness of this process is because corrosion is not taking place during washing and that the release of chloride is diffusion controlled (Turgoose S 1982 :97-101).

b. Heat Treatment Methods

Heat treatment method for archaeological iron artifact was first proposed by Eriksen and Thegel, where heating alone in air was used for removal of chlorides by their volatilization at high temperatures. But later on Arrhenius et. al. and North and Pearson found that reducing atmosphere was more suitable for the removal of chlorides, reduction of iron oxides and prevention of oxidation of the cementite and ferrite of the metal core.

Barker, Kendell and O' shea (1980) , on analysis of the corrosion products on archaeological iron artifacts, found that the main compounds present were ferric oxyhydroxide ,ferrous oxide, ferrous and ferric chloride and ferrous sulphate together with some sodium chloride (Clarke, R.W. and Blackshaw, S.M.).

North in 1988 suggested that the reaction of chlorides of marine iron artifacts when heated at 400 ^{o}C in air will behave similar to a mixture consisting of mainly Ferrous Oxy chloride FeOCl with smaller amounts of ferrous chloride $FeCl_2$ and ferric chloride $FeCl_3$ (North N.A 1988). This does not prove that Ferrous oxy chloride FeOCl is present in marine iron corrosion product. The reactions occurring as:

$$4\ FeOCl + O_2 \rightarrow 2\ Fe_2O_3 + 2Cl_2$$
$$3\ FeOCl \rightarrow Fe_2O_3 + FeCl_3$$
$$4\ FeCl_2 + 3O_2 \rightarrow 2\ Fe_2O_3 + 4Cl_2$$

At the temperature of 400°C ferrous chloride $FeCl_2$ which has boiling point around 294°C, being in a gaseous stage will be expelled from the artifact. So theoretically, if an artifact is heated at 400 - 500 °C , then removal of all chlorides from the artifact should be achieved. But in reality conversion of ferrous chloride $FeCl_2$ to ferric chloride $FeCl_3$ is not complete. Near the residual metal core it is difficult for oxygen to reach in innermost corrosponding layer (i.e. creating oxygen deficiency in the innermost corrosion layers) and, thus no oxidation takes place. If this residual ferric chloride $FeCl_3$ is not removed, it will corrode the residual metal core. To remove this residual ferric chloride $FeCl_3$ artifact must be heated to above 670 °C . This is sublimation temperature of ferric chloride $FeCl_3$. Heating the iron artifacts in air also gives secondary reactions which can be represented as:

$$4\ FeC + 13O_2 \rightarrow 6Fe_2O_3 + 4CO_2$$
$$4\ Fe + 3O_2 \rightarrow 2Fe_2O_3$$

The oxidation of cementite (FeC) is found to be maximum at 450°c and above this temperature practically no cementite is left in the iron. These two secondary or side reactions are very harmful to the artifact. Because of the increase in the volumes few the corrosion products resulting from these reactions the bond between corrosion products and the residual metal is weakened. This leads to the corrosion products becoming crumbly and spalling off the artifact. If this happens to cast iron artifacts containing important markings and inscriptions on the corrosion layer, then the artifact is completely lost. Due to the severe drawbacks in heating of iron in air, the method has been modified and instead heating or reduction of the iron is brought about in the presence of hydrogen or a mixture of nitrogen and hydrogen gas.

On the temperature between 100°C to 300 °C the ferric oxy chloride and ferric chloride are converted in ferrous chloride which can be represented as:

$$FeCl_3 + H_2O \rightarrow FeOCl + 2\ HCl$$
$$10\ FeOCl + 3H_2 \rightarrow 2Fe_3O_4 + 4FeCl_2 + 2\ HCl + 2H_2O$$

At the temperature of 350°C, hydrogen reduces to $FeCl_2$ and iron oxides.

$$FeCl_2 + 2H_2 \rightarrow Fe + 2HCl$$

This reaction starts at temperature of 300 °C and is faster at 400 °C temperature. In the case of reduction of iron oxides by hydrogen (North N.A 1988:207-254). Below 570 °C, FeO is directly reduced to metallic iron, without formation of wustite (FeO) at any stage.

$$Fe_3O_4 + 2H_2O \rightarrow 3\ Fe + 4H_2O$$

Above the 570 °C temperature the reduction of FeO to metallic iron is found to be occurring in two stages. They can be represented as:

$$Fe_3O_4 + H_2 \rightarrow 3FeO + H_2O$$
$$FeO + H_2 \rightarrow Fe + H_2O$$

At 400 °C the reduction of FeO to metallic iron is possible only if pure hydrogen, with a high flow rate through the furnace is used. (North N.A 1988:207-254).

Theoretically, in presence of pure dry hydrogen complete volatilization of chlorides and metallic ion only 90% chloride production should be achieved at 400 °C. But in practice only 90% chloride volatilization has been observed. This is because the innermost layers are least breathed, arising due to the relatively slow diffusion of gases through the pores of the corrosion layer.

For complete removal of chlorides from the iron artifact a temperature of 700 °C or more is required. If sodium chloride is also present, then 850 °C or more is needed for its volatilization.

In this method of treatment of the artifacts of cast iron, in addition to complete removal of chloride ions, consolidates or hardens the graphitized zones. The porosity of the corrosion products layer is also increased to a large extent as conversion of iron oxides to metallic iron occur on heating. It was observed in the 17th to 19th century the cast and wrought iron heated at the temperature 600 °C or above cause damage to the metallurgical structure (North Owens and Pearson 1976:192-197 and North N.A. and Pearson C. 1977:146-157). A treatment temperature at least 60 hours at 400 °C temperature was found to be safe for both cast and wrought iron artifacts without any change in their metallurgical structures. Nowadays two different approaches to hydrogen furnace treatment of iron are more commonly used. Hydrogen reduction at 700-900 °C temperature in a stream of nitrogen and hydrogen mixture and heating of iron below 400 °C temperature in pure hydrogen and washing in sodium hydroxide solution to remove the residual chloride.

i. Hydrogen Reduction at 700 °C - 900 °C

It was developed by Barkman et. al. in the 1960s. The principle behind this reduction is temperature about 850 °C at which all the chlorides in the corrosion products layer are volatilized thus stabilizing the artifacts. The loosely adhering soils and bulk of concretions are removed so as to improve the free circulation of cracker gas over the metal surface. The artifact is secured to the base and clamped down over it so as to ensure an air tight seal. The ammonia cracker is allowed to reach at the temperature of 850 °C which is the operating temperature. Nitrogen is passed through the retort so as to displace all traces of air which if not removed completely would lead to an explosion on introduction of hydrogen into the system. The cracker gas, mixture of hydrogen and nitrogen is introduced into the retort in place of the nitrogen gas. The furnace is then heated up to 850 °C. The heating is gradual and the rate adopted is such that 850 °C is reached in 20 hours, to avoid thermal shock. After heating for 100 hours the cracking gas is replaced by nitrogen gas, allowing the furnace temperature to fall down to room temperature. The system is kept at room temperature for 48 hours. The artifact is then removed from the retort and coated with a preservative coating of two pack epoxy varnish or a low bake vinyl lacquer either by vacuum impregnation for small artifact and for large artifact applied leniently by brush .

The most important drawback of this method is that the metallurgical structure of the artifact subjected to high temperatures i.e. 850°C, is irreversibly altered. As metallurgical structure is an important record of the smelting and forging processes used during the manufacture of the artifacts, these evidences are lost during this process.

For totally rusted archaeological cast iron, the loss of information due to treatment at 800 °C will not be great and there seems to be little objection to the use of hydrogen reduction method for this purpose (Tylecote R.F. and Black J.W.B 1980:187-196).During treatment of cast iron artifacts by this method, apparent melting of iron at surprisingly low temperatures (800 °C - 900 °C) occurs. This completely destroys to artifact (North N.A 1988:207-254) .

ii. Heating of iron artifacts below 400 °C and simple washing

The principle of this method is the partial removal of chlorides from 6-9% to 1-2% by heating the artifact at 400 °C in a hydrogen reducing atmosphere (North N.A 1988:207-254). Due to the reduction of iron oxides to metallic iron the porosity of the corrosion products is greatly increased, resulting in the increase in the rate of chloride release into the wash solution, sodium hydroxide. Simple washing immediately follows hydrogen furnace reduction.

The electrical furnace used here must have provision for heating in a stream of hydrogen or nitrogen. After putting the iron artifact in the furnace, its temperature is slowly raised. Firstly at 120 °C all entrapped water is removed by evaporation. The temperature is then gradually raised up to 400 °C in a stream of pure dry hydrogen. Care must be exercised as in the above method not to allow mixing of oxygen with the hydrogen gas. The rate of the hydrogen flow is set at 1/10 of the furnace insert volume per minute, in order to have an efficient reduction. It means a high flow rate is kept during the process. The system is kept at this temperature for

48 hours then brought down to 100 °C when the hydrogen flow is replaced by pure dry nitrogen flow.

When the temperature is reached at room temperature the cooling become continued .The furnace open immediately then artifact immediately immersed into a solution of 2% sodium hydroxide .The washing of residual chloride is done following the simple washing method.

The washing part of this method which may take between 8 to 40 weeks lengthen. But this method is safer than high temperature methods as the metallurgical structure is not altered if treated for less than 60 hours. Any iron artifact which has been cold worked should not be treated by this method. Cast iron treated by this method finds the mechanical strength of its graphitized zone to have largely increased and it becomes much less prone to physical damage (North N.A 1988:207-254). The very adherent and hard concretions are converted to a crumbly friable mass .Which is easily removed by brushing. Unlike electrolysis no electrical contact is made to the artifact, so one source of damage is eliminated. In case of iron artifacts microcrystalline cosmolloid wax is more acceptable.

c. Electrolysis

The aim of this method is the reduction of ferric oxy hydroxide FeOOH to FeO by alkaline sulphite reduction. This reduction changes is responsible for the increase in the porosity of the corrosion products, consequently increasing the rate of chloride ions diffusion into the solution.

$$3\ FeOOH + 4H + e^- \rightarrow Fe(OH)_3 + 2\ H_2O$$

The electron required to bring about the reduction reaction is supplied by an external applied voltage. Cast iron corrosion products do not show any evidence of metallic iron formation after electrolytic reduction. Once the reduction of magnetite is completed further passage of electric current is utilized for the evolution of hydrogen gas only.

The artifact can clean by removing the bulk of the concretion. After removal of the bulk of concretion placed in the middle of electrolytic container. Small artifacts are suspended from a rod placed across the top of the container and for the large artifacts mild steel cradles can be used as support. The anodes are placed around the artifact at a distance between 20 and 80 cm, except for the steel rod- anode, placed in the center of the artifact, where the distance between the anode and the artifact is only 3 to 10 cm (North N.A 1988:207-254). Anodes should be well secured to avoid any accidental contract with the artifact. Anodes are connected to the positive terminal of the D.C. power source while the artifact to the negative terminal. The water level should be 10 cm above the artifact (North N.A 1988:207-254). In case of cast iron, solid sodium hydroxide is added to the water so as to make a 0.5 M sodium hydroxide solution whereas for wrought iron the sodium hydroxide solution should be 0.1M.

A suitable current and voltage depending on the artifacts to be treated is applied to start the electrolysis. The current can be applied intermittently on the basis of 8 weeks on and 8 weeks off, or continuously for eight weeks after which the artifact is taken out of the bath and any residual concretions, which come out easily to remove.

The large artifacts should be occasionally rotated during treatment, so as to treat the regions in contact with the support stand equally. During the course of electrolytic reduction, the chloride extraction is monitored and the electrolyte, sodium hydroxide solution is changed as soon as the amount of chloride in it reaches 2000 ppm. When the level of chloride in the electrolyte becomes negligible or constant the artifact is then removed from the electrolytic bath and transferred to 2% sodium hydroxide solution where it undergoes simple washing to remove the chloride ions. After chloride removal by this method is complete, and then the artifact is immersed in distilled water to remove excess of sodium hydroxide from the artifact in the same manner as in simple washing.

The mild steel, stainless steel or glass can be use for electrolytic container. Plastic container are avoidable because they rapidly become brittle and crack. In order to avoid the artifacts to come into contact with the sides or bottom of a container consisting of conducting material, insulating materials can be placed between the artifact and support stand as well as between the stand and the container.

Hydrogen and oxygen gas with some sodium hydroxide mist is evolved during electrolysis. To suppress the mist evolution, detergent can be added to the electrolyte or its surface can be covered with polystyrene beads. The surface area of an anode must be bigger but not smaller than the surfaced area of the artifacts under treatment (Organ R.M 1978 and1973). Anodes can be of mild steel sheets reinforced along the bottom edge of anodes in order to prevent them from coming into contact with walls of metal container.

To get good electric contact with the electric cable with wrought iron artifact, a small part of its surface is scrubbed and clean of all corrosion products with a steel wire brush and the electric wire is firmly clamped to the metal. In case of cast iron artifacts, a hole is drilled through the graphitized zone up to the residual metal core, then with a smaller diameter drill bit, a hole of 10 to 30 mm is made into the metal core. A cylindrical mild steel rod is introduced into the hole and the cathodic cable wire is attached to it.

To start the electrolysis and preparation of electrolyte solution the tap water can be used. But later on when the quantity of chloride released from the artifact becomes comparable to the amount of chloride in tap water, then it is replaced by de-ionized water. For electrolysis of marine iron artifacts, the best electrolyte appears to be aqueous sodium hydroxide (North N.A 1988:207-254). Sodium carbonate is less caustic and much safer so it can also be used. It is less conductive than sodium hydroxide and higher concentrations, 5 to 8% by weight must be used. Sodium carbonate is being less soluble in water than sodium hydroxide , considerable effort is necessary to dissolve large amounts needed for the electrolysis of large artifact. The mild steel corrode faster at low pH provided by sodium carbonate and thus has to be replaced faster than in case of sodium hydroxide when used as electrolyte.

For the wrought iron artifact the D.C. source should be able to supply 150 A at 6 V while for cast iron it should be 20 A at 3 V. Large number of wrought iron artifacts can be treated simultaneously in one or different containers using the same transformer rectifier while cast iron artifacts must be treated individually. Cast and wrought iron artifacts should not be treated simultaneously or in separate containers using the same transformer- rectifier. The different voltage applied for wrought and cast iron artifacts. For wrought iron a voltage of approximately 5 V has been found to produce good results. But for cast iron which requires a gentle electrolysis in order to preserve the gradphitized layer, voltage applied must be just enough to produce hydrogen evolution.

If once a cast iron artifacts have dried out, electrolysis should never be attempted on it, as in the drying process, fresh corrosion will have taken place at the graphitized layer and un-corroded metal interface, and formed a parting layer in between them (Organ R.M 1978). During electrolysis due to hydrogen evolution the corroded layers can be mechanically disrupted and this may lead to crumbling down of the artifact. Wrought iron is affected and cannot be retained. Only artifact having enough solid metal core and a shape should be treated by electrolysis. Artifact heavily corroded and not very strong when treated can be reduced to a lump of metal.

1. Indoor Electrolysis :

i. Electrochemical cleaning

The corrosion of metal is an electrochemical reaction. The electrochemical and electrolytic reduction cleaning processes are the most common techniques utilized to halt, stabilize, and even reverse the oxidation of the metal. Hamilton 1976:30-49 and North 1987:223-227, given a detailed discussion of electrolytic reduction. In the conservation literature it is the general practice to distinguish between electrochemical and electrolytic cleaning.

Conservation Reaction

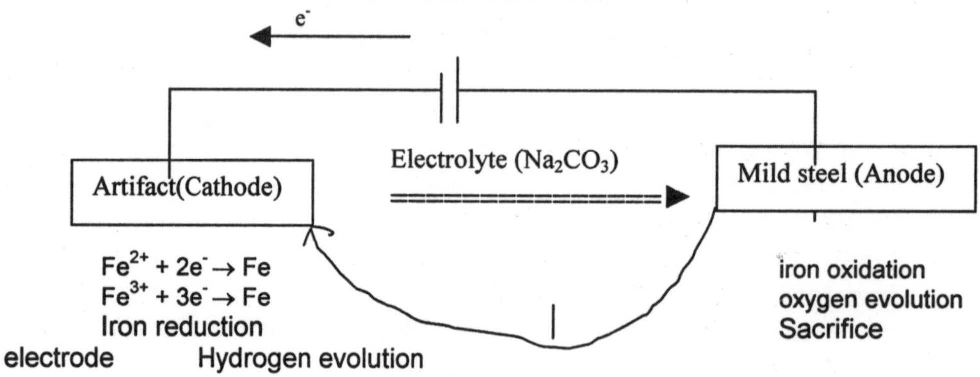

In fact both techniques are electrochemical reactions based on the couple of two metals occupying different positions on the galvanic or electromotive series of the metals without an externally applied electromotive force (EMF) and the latter is an electrochemical reaction maintained by an externally applied electromotive force EMF or electric current. Both cleaning techniques are described in the various literatures. Plenderleith 1956 is a source often cited. While useful information is provided by Plenderleith and Torraca 1968 and Plenderleith and Werner 1971, a more thorough coverage is desirable to realize the maximum potential and benefits of these techniques.

ii. Galvanic cleaning

This technique is applied in the conservation of marine recovered iron artifacts . Only this technique recommended in two frequently cited works on underwater archeology (Marx 1971:125 Peterson 1969:83-84). Electrochemical cleaning is not a desirable alternative for marine-recovered iron artifacts which are deeply chloride contaminated. For iron from terrestrial sites often not desirable electrochemical cleaning. Since chlorides present in iron is not a real problems. In this reference the statement and comment of Noël Hume's 1969: "Those amateurs who have been told that it is a simple method that can readily be performed on the kitchen stove are advised to forget it." To be effective, galvanic cleaning requires that a substantial metal core be present in the artifact is to being treated. For the cleaning of few small artifacts this process can be recommended . Galvanic cleaning is considered as an obsolete technique. Some of its advantages and its major disadvantages are presented. Galvanic cleaning involves placing the iron artifact in a container and surrounding it with a much more active anodic metal, such as zinc or aluminum, and filling the container with an electrolyte. In this process, nascent hydrogen acts as the reducing agent as it evolves from the surface of the iron artifact. The chlorides are removed and reduced iron artifact is left by the reaction. It is necessary to control the electrode potential of the artifact being treated and to be effective. In galvanic cleaning, this is determined by the couple between the two metals and by the electrolyte. The simplest form of galvanic cleaning consists of wrapping the artifact loosely in aluminum foil and placing it in a glass beaker of 10% sodium hydroxide or a 10 to 20% solution of sodium carbonate. Noël Hume (1969:283) suggested the using an electrolyte of sodium bicarbonate. The artifact is left in the caustic solution until the aluminum foil completely oxidizes. The reaction can be speeded up by heating the solution. The artifact is then rinsed and the process is repeated until satisfactory results are achieved. The main demerit is that only small, lightly corroded artifact can be treated by this process.

The most commonly used form of galvanic reduction differs from the above only in that granulated zinc or aluminum granules are used to cover the artifact and a 10 to 20% solution of sodium hydroxide is employed (Plenderleith and Torraca 1968:241 and Plenderleith and Werner 1971:194-197). Since heating accelerates the process, metal pans, or heat resistant glassware, are recommended. Ideally the solution is heated to boiling, and the level of the solution is maintained with the addition of distilled water. The cleaning continues until the electrolyte is exhausted or the activity of the zinc diminishes. The process is repeated with fresh or cleaned zinc and fresh caustic soda until all the materials are reduced and all traces of chlorides have been eliminated. This is determined by qualitative test for chloride. If high levels of chlorides are allowed to remain, future outbreaks of corrosion are inevitable. The process requires facilities to heat the container, and an adequate ventilation system, such as a fume hood, to exhaust the caustic vapors. In the reduction process the caustic solution is exhausted and has to be periodically discarded, and considerable zinc is lost through oxidation. The activity of the remaining zinc is considerably reduced by an accumulated film of oxychloride and carbonate. To be renewed, the zinc must be cleaned with dilute hydrochloric acid solutions rinsed in distilled water and then dried (Plenderleith and Werner 1971:196) or melted in a ladle under a reducing flame and re-granulated by slowly pouring into water (Organ 1973:193). In the latter, the reducing flame is going to have to be very good to remove oxychloride and carbonate and each time the zinc is reclaimed, slag formation will further reduce the quantity of zinc.

The galvanic cleaning process is impractical for iron artifacts with extensive chloride corrosion compounds. The artifact is always obscured and it is not possible to follow visually its progress. Even under ideal conditions the process requires constant supervision and is messy. The fumes produced are obnoxious and are irritating to the skin, the eyes, and the throat. Also, it is often difficult to provide simultaneously adequate ventilation and adequate heat. Any large artifact, especially chloride-contaminated, require a long processing time and a prohibitive amount of zinc, which has to be constantly re-cleaned and replenished. In sum, galvanic cleaning of most metal artifacts should be considered only if equipment for electrolytic reduction is unavailable, and even then it may be a waste of time for a lot of iron artifacts, especially if they are very large.

iii. Electrolytic Reduction Cleaning

The electrolytic reduction cleaning is one of the most valuable tools for conservators. It can be selected exclusively for its mechanical cleaning action of the evolved hydrogen for the reduction process. This process can be used for most of iron artifacts. Efficient electrolytic reduction, however, involves more than wiring up artifacts for electrolysis. For performing the work of conservation of iron artifacts the knowledge of corrosion processes and electrochemical thermodynamics is essential. Conservator must be familiar with electrode potentials and pH and also to know how these variables relate to electrode corrosion, passivation, and immunity. When dealing with chloride-contaminated iron artifacts these factors are crucial. A good knowledge enables the conservator to understand and better control what is going on in the electrolytic cell and to correct adverse conditions and this is not to say that satisfactory results cannot be obtained by the novice conservators. This technique involves in setting up an electrolytic cell with the artifact to be cleaned as the cathode. An electrolytic cell consists of a compartment or container with two electrodes; the anode and the cathode and containing a suitable electrically conducting solution called the electrolyte. The oxidation and reduction is due to electric current from an external direct current power supplied to the system. On the anodic side oxidation occurs and oxygen is evolved. The anode is the positive terminal of the electrolytic cell on which electrons, negatively charged ions or colloidal particles, travel when an electric current is passed through the cell. The cathode is the negative terminal of an electrolytic cell to which positively charged of metallic ions travel and reduction takes place and hydrogen is evolved. In the reduction process some of the positively charged metal ions in the compounds on the surface of the artifact are reduced to a metallic state in situ . In addition, chlorides and other anions are drawn from the iron artifacts and migrate toward the positively charged anode by electrolytic attraction.

The main advantage of electrolytic reduction is that the externally applied electromotive force (EMF) or electric current provides the conservator with considerable flexibility. The current density is to be controlled. This control enables a low current density that creates a pre-selected electrode potential conducive for the consolidation or reduction of some mineralized metals. If there is an underlying metal core then it is theoretically possible to reduce enough of the ferrous corrosion compounds back to a metallic state through electrolytic reduction. After eliminating the chloride components consolidate the corrosion layer. On the same way a high current density can be applied so that the evolved hydrogen will mechanically remove completely oxidized crust. When using electrolytic reduction cleaning, the procedural factors to be considered are the equipment and the experimental variables.

a. Equipments for Electrolytic Reduction Cleaning

For the removal of chloride from the archaeological iron artifacts by electrolytic reduction following equipment are required

i. Terminal Wires and Clips
ii. Anodic Material
iii. Electrolyte Container
iv. Power Supply

During the electrolytic reduction cleaning the function of equipments

i. Terminal Wires and Clips

The maximum rating insulated copper wire can be used for the most artifacts. This wire is the standard two-ply multistranded wire commonly found on many electrical appliances. The wire is quite flexible and easy to use. One strand of the wire is used for the negative connection, the other one for the positive connection. For the larger artifacts more current is required which may supply by multistranded wire. Copper wire is recommended because it has a larger current capacity. There should be check the amperage capacity of the wire before using. Thumb rule may be follow during electrolysis. Steel alligator test and battery clips can be used to attach the terminal leads to the artifact and the anode. For taking down artifacts in electrolysis the appropriate size clips on the terminals should be facilitate. The selection of the size of the clip is determined by the current to be used and size of the artifact. Steel clips usually are cadmium or zinc-plated and should be stripped of this plating by a quick bath in a dilute solution of hydrochloric acid. If it left in the acid for long time, the tempered steel spring is weakened and breaks when depressed. The removal of the cadmium or zinc coating prevents any plating of this metal from the anode clips onto the artifact. For the same reason, copper clips should not be used. Copper clips on the positive terminal, like the exposed copper wire attached to the anode clips, eventually go into anodic dissolution when submerged in the electrolyte, and plates onto the cathode. In order to prevent the anodic dissolution, the exposed copper wire should be coated with an acrylic, polyvinyl acetate or silicone rubber.

ii. Anodic Material

For electrolytic cleaning of iron artifact sixteen gages expanded mild steel mesh with half-inch openings can be used. This type of materials is efficient for anode. This mesh is readily cut, relatively flexible, easy to form-fit around the artifact and does not trap any gas. This mesh does not conceal the artifact from view and permits free circulation of the electrolyte. Mild steel container can serve as the container and the anodic material. Mild steel anodes are surprisingly durable. As long as an adequate alkaline pH (minimum of 8.5) is maintained at the surface of the mild steel anode, it is less susceptible to chloride corrosion and will even outlast stainless steel. To circulate the electrolyte, it is necessary to maintain this level of alkalinity. Therefore, mild steel anodes are commonly used as the oxygen-hydrogen cell electrodes.

Stainless steel makes a superior anode and it is often recommended because it is relatively inert . All stainless steels do not make equally suitable anodic material. A stainless steel with a high percentage of chromium and nickel or even titanium needs to be selected. Particularly serviceable type stainless steel is composed of 16 to 18% chromium and 10 to 14% nickel and 2-3% molybdenum may be selected for anode.

For resists to chloride corrosion only serviceable type stainless steel can be selected. It is a good alternative to mild steel anodes in an alkaline electrolyte.

As long as the hydroxyl ion concentration in the electrolyte is kept high, one will get better service from mild steel anodes than stainless steel. In any case, when either is used, it is much simpler and more economical to change the electrolyte before the chlorides build up to such an extent that they alter the pH and electrode potential at the anode, destroying the anode's passivity and causing it to go into dissolution. The anode has to be replaced when this type of dissolution happens. When stainless steel or mild steel anodes are used then electrolyte should be regularly replaced and using a chloride-monitoring system as a guide.

iii. Electrolyte Container

A container is used in an electrolytic setup. It is non-conductive and many kinds of nonconductive caustic and acid-resistant materials such as polyvinyl chloride, polypropylene and polyethylene. Glass containers may also be used. The variety and range of potentially satisfactory containers are obviously broad. For small artifacts, a common coffee can, with the can used as the container and the anode is as effective as anything much more elaborated. In addition to non-conducting containers, conducting mild steel containers have a definite place in electrolytic cleaning. The metal container serves as a part of the anode and may be substituted for any of the electrolytic setups .The "T"-shaped container is constructed in two parts as the stem and the cross. Each of which is open at one end. When these parts are joined then containers is used to clean artifact with auxiliary sheets of expanded mild steel near the top surface to achieve a better distribution of current. Separated, the two are employed to clean an assortment of large iron artifacts. After all artifacts can cleaned, the two containers bolted together, placed on a "T" arrangement of stoves to rinse the artifacts, other breechblocks, and an artifact in alternate boiling-cooling de-ionized water. With the final sealant with microcrystalline wax, the water is drained and replaced. It is not necessary to dry the artifacts before heating up the wax, for the temperature of the wax is taken to over 300°F which is well above the boiling point of water; thus all residual moisture is vaporized in the wax impregnation step. Mild steel containers can be constructed in vaiious gauges. It is durable and versatile, even in the lighter gauges. For maximum life, use a gage that provides the strength as required. Containers which can be employed in any of the described setup alternatives in combination with auxiliary anodes to assure a more even distribution of current. Metal containers has a distinct advantage over plastic containers. All stages of the conservation process can be carried out in them. This is especially advantageous for very large artifact, where it is not economically feasible to have different containers for electrolysis, rinsing/dehydration and wax impregnation.

A welded mild steel container is used for large artifacts. They can be constructed very economically, and will last for years. North (1987:225) stated that , "If mild steel tanks are being used on no account should these be made the anode, in the presence of chloride ions, this causes corrosion particularly at weld lines and bends in the metal." When corrosion takes place at the stress points such as weld seams and bends. After years, one welded mild steel containers, developed a series of leaks along the seams. Steel drums, barrels, paint cans may be use for electrolysis purposes. Thus North's recommendation should be ignored, but the precautions of not using a sodium carbonate electrolyte and using 5% sodium hydroxide instead of 2% sodium hydroxide for the first 2 or 3 baths when cleaning a large iron artifacts with high chloride content should be taken. In addition, it is difficult to understand how a metal containers can be isolated from the anodes, and even if it is done, the chloride ions are still present which will still attack the metal containers , but if the containers is not hooked up as the anode, it is not anodically passivated which affords it some protection. The recommendation by North is totally disregarded by most conservator responsible for treating large iron artifacts. Care must be taken to insure that the metal anode containers remain passive during electrolysis; otherwise, the metal will go into anodic dissolution and create perforations, which are difficult to repair. This is sometimes difficult when using low current density electrolysis in the presence of high levels of chloride ions; however most of the difficulties can be overcome if a 5% sodium hydroxide electrolyte is used until the chloride levels decrease or the current density can be increased to keep the anode passive. A few comments should be made concerning the safety of using metal containers and the anode. Most of direct current power supplies used in electrolytic cleaning operate in a 6 to 12 or a 24 to 32-volt range and a 0 to 50 or 0 to 200-amperage range, but the actual voltage utilized is only 3 to 6 volts. Amperage means micro unit of current flow through electrolyte from the direct power of current power supply. As per per thumb rule that less than 32 volts is not hazardous because the IR (current resistance) drop in the human body is such that little or no current would pass. Care should be taken, however, to avoid shorting the two terminals of the higher voltage power supplies against each other.

iv. Power Supplies for electrolytic reduction

The laboratory should have well-equipped for the removal of chloride from the iron artifacts by electrolytic reduction process. During the process D.C. power supply is require to regulate electrolytic reduction. The power units fall into four general current ranges and are capable of cleaning any artifact from a small to a large size of artifact. The small D.C. power supplies have an output current with less than 0.1% ripple when larger power supplies, battery chargers, have more than 0.5% ripple. The low ripple power supplies are recommended for well-controlled reduction; however a little ripple is not harmful. Ripples means decrease in resistance in wire which are used for power supply. According to the size of the artifact and number of artifacts on any unit select the power supple depends upon the desired control. These provide a means of determining and adjusting the current as the treatment progresses. During electrolysis of the iron the current increases as the metallic species are reduced and the resistance of the artifact and the electrolyte decreases. Due to increase in chloride and other ions in the electrolyte the I R (current resistance) drop is formed. The drop is the decreasing in current i.e. flow of electron on reverse direction. This is the main reason for the current increase; the decrease in the resistance of the artifact plays only a minor role. If an artifact is to be electrolytically reduced at a fixed current density or a predetermined electrode potential then variable adjustments are necessary.

Battery chargers can be employed. Battery chargers, however, are not designed to run continuously for electrolytic cleaning. If they are to be utilized in electrolysis it is usually necessary to remove timers, relays and charging rate devices to make them serviceable. Anyone with a basic knowledge of electrical circuits can easily alter most direct current battery chargers for electrolytic cleaning of iron artifacts.

Since an electrolytic cell for cleaning artifacts shortage the resistance of a battery and the battery chargers generally do not have the necessary internal resistance controls to compensate for it. The chargers run well above their maximum safe operating amperage. Additional resistance must be added to the circuits to keep them from overheating. Variable autotransformers is automatically adjust itself from primary to secondary i.e. high to low vice versa for voltage supply for this purpose , such as power starts on the input alternating current line and variable rheostats or line resistors on the outgoing direct current negative terminals serve for this purpose. The conservator who has basic knowledge of electronics can successfully modifies battery chargers and other D.C. power supplies can be modified easily for the purposes of conservation. The easiest procedure is to add a variable autotransformer to the input-alternating current circuit. This allows the full amperage range of the unit, from 0 to 200 amps, to be used.

b. Chloride monitoring during electrolytic reduction

For crucial to the efficiency and success of electrolytic reduction of iron artifact is a system to monitor the chloride concentration quantitatively in the electrolyte. There are several such type of tests exist for chloride determination. The Mohr method and ion specific electrode are often used, but the mercuric nitrate titration method is suggested because of its simplicity.

i. Determination of Chloride by Mercuric Nitrate Method

To quantitative determination of chloride or sodium chloride in parts per million in an aqueous solution the mercuric nitrate test method is used. It is a quick and simple test to quantitative determination of chloride or sodium chloride and gives accurate results. For the complexometric titration for chloride determination the following procedure and equipments are used;

Equipments

- Two 25 ml. burettes; preferably one automatic.
- Two small plastic bottles with droppers.
- 250 ml. beakers.
- A magnetic stirrer.
- Teflon-coated stirring bars.
- Two 500 ml. plastic bottles.

Chemicals

- Diphenylcarbazone-bromophenol blue indicator
- 0.02N mercuric nitrate solution.
- 18N sulphuric acid (keep to refill each burette).
- Nitric acid to clean the stirring bars.

ii. Procedure

Take a 20 ml. sample of electrolyte or solution to be tested, and place it in a 250 ml glass beaker. Place the beaker on the magnetic stirrer and put a Teflon stirring bar in the beaker. Adjust the stirrer until the liquid is in a steady swirl. Add five drops of diphenylcarbazone-bromophenol blue indicator. This will change the colour of the solution to blue. Add drops of sulphuric acid (usually 18N sulfuric acid for sodium hydroxide electrolyte, 9N sulfuric acid for sodium carbonate electrolyte, or 4.5N sulphuric acid for water solutions) from the burette or with an eye dropper until an acid end point is reached. The acid end point is indicated by a colour change form blue to clear. The amount of sulphuric acid does not need to be measured; it only acidifies the sample for the next step.

Titrate 0.02N mercuric nitrate, drop by drop, from the automatic burette until the sample reaches a violet end point. The colour changes gradually from clear to violet. Near the end point, each drop will show a flash of colour. Continue until a single drops swirls into a single even violet colour through out the solution. Additional drops make the colour more intense, but do not change it. Note the amount of mercuric nitrate titrated to reach the end point. The concentration of chloride or sodium chloride in parts per million is calculated by the following formulas.

$T \times N \times 0.05846 \times 1{,}000{,}000$
$20 = T \times N \times 2923 =$ ppm NaCl
$T \times N \times 0\ .03545 \times 1{,}000{,}000$
$20 = T \times N \times 1772.5 =$ ppm Chloride
T= amount of mercuric nitrate titrated.
N = normality of mercuric nitrate

The sensitivity of the titration can be increase by using a smaller normality solution or decreased by using a larger normality solution of mercuric nitrate. Adjustments can also be made for larger or smaller sample sizes. After mixing the new solutions, there should be calibrated against a known standard.

The NaCl readings are used to check the reagents against a known solution of sodium chloride. The test gives the total amount of chloride ions or sodium chloride in the electrolyte. However, the unused alkaline electrolyte has a certain amount of chlorides in it. What needs to be measured are the chlorides expelled from the artifact. To do this, the same test is run on a sample of unused electrolyte. This provides a blank which is subtracted from the sample from the electrolytic bath. Example: If a sample takes 2 ml. of mercuric nitrate to reach the end point, then 11.7 ppm chloride ions is present; if the blank is 8.7 then the amount of chlorides derived from the artifact is 2.9. Since the reagents are unstable they should be tested weekly against a known sodium chloride solution to assure consistency.

In taking the electrolyte samples, separate clean beakers should be used for each sample or the beakers should be rinsed with de-ionized water between each sample. Different stirring rods should be used with each sample or rinsed between samples. The stirring rods become stained purple but can be cleaned by putting them in dilute solution of nitric acid. Through this whole process, it should always be kept in mind that the glassware must be kept clean and uncontaminated at all times. After thoroughly washing the glassware, they should be rinsed with de-ionized water to avoid any cross contamination.

In the chloride testing procedure there should be consider; The diphenylcarbazone -bromophenol end point is to some degree subjective, but most individual are consistent about their end point. If only one individual familiar with it should the tests then more reliable and consistent results are obtained. All the chemicals at the exact concentration required for the chloride test. Dilute reagent grade sulphuric acid with an equal volume of distilled or de-ionized water. Slowly add the acid to the water, never the water to the acid otherwise extreme heat will be generated.

For preparation of 0.02N Mercuric Nitrate Solution, $Hg(NO_3)_2 \cdot H_2O$. Dissolve 3.42 grams of reagent grade mercuric nitrate to 1 liter of distilled or de-ionized water and for preparation of diphenylcarbazone-bromophenol blue indicator. Dissolve 0.5 grams of reagent grade crystalline diphenylcarbazone and 0 .05 grams of crystalline bromophenol blue in 100 milliliters of 95% ethanol. While this may be mixed, the weight is so small, 1000 ppm sodium chloride solution to test reagents. Dissolve one gram sodium chloride in one liter of distilled or de-ionized water. It may be diluted in half for 500 ppm sodium chloride and again diluted a second time for 250 ppm.

It is possible to determine how the chloride removal is progressing by quantitatively measuring of the chloride concentration in parts per million in a sample of the electrolyte. The chloride level should be regularly and frequently, at least once a week, calculated and recorded. These data can be used to make a graph that visually depicts at a glance the cleaning progress of an artifact. This will save much valuable time and enable the conservator to determine when to change a chloride-contaminated electrolyte and when all the detectable soluble chlorides have been removed from the artifact. The systematic chloride monitoring assures that each artifact remains in electrolysis for the minimum amount of time. Chloride monitoring is essential for evaluating the efficiency of chloride removal from the artifact during treatment. It measures the chlorides going into solution from the artifact and is used to determine when this process is completed. Chloride monitoring cannot be used to determine the efficiency of the reduction of the iron compounds. To determine the efficiency of the reduction of the iron compounds can only be confirmed with analytical tests on samples taken from the artifact before and after treatment.

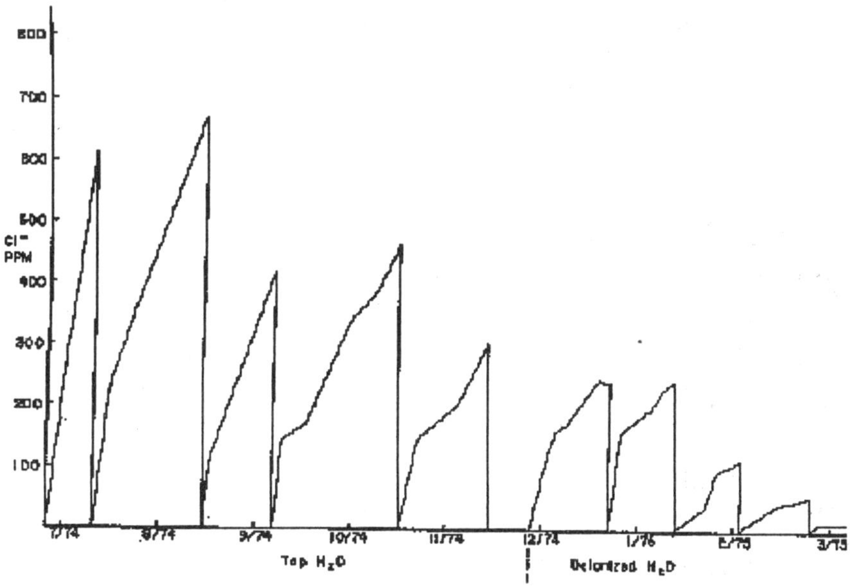

The progress of chloride diffusion in a typical iron artifact

The above graphical data shows that initially chlorides coming from the artifact are high and thereafter decreases as the electrolyte is periodically changed. Drops in the graph to the zero line represent electrolyte changes. The two-week gap in the graph when the artifact has taken out of electrolysis to mechanically clean the remaining encrustation and loose corrosion products. Occasionally a drop from a previous is high as seen on chloride graphs, especially when the chloride level is high. Perhaps this is caused by chlorides reacting with corrosion products from the anode, chlorate formation, or the actual liberation of chlorine which causes the chlorides to be undetectable by taking them out of solution. Electrolysis is continued until the chloride concentration levels off for several days and does not increase above that present in a blank of the electrolyte.

C. Electrolytic setup for Conservation of Iron Artifacts

1. Type of Electrolytic setups

The manner in which artifacts are set up for electrolysis is dependent upon :

The size and condition of the artifact; The backlog of artifacts waiting to be processed; The control of direct current power supplies by regulating devices ;The current capacities ;The number, size and nature of the containers.

It is commonly described in the literature about electrolytic setup (Plenderleith 1956:194-196; Plenderleith and Torraca 1968:243; Plenderleith and Werner 1971:198). Hamilton stated that each alternative has its disadvantages and advantages.

The "Ideal" electrolytic setup as shown in figure consists of one artifact, surrounded by a close, form-fitted anode that is equidistant from all surfaces of the artifact, in one container and on one regulated direct current power supply.

A conservator is able to control the current to the artifact and to maintain a pre-determined electrode potential conducive to metal reduction on the surface of the artifact by this setup. It also allows to monitor the chloride level in the electrolyte as it comes out of a single artifact. This option is selected when it is important to the optimum conditions to preserve those artifacts that are especially significant and need to be conserved as carefully as possible. Because a separate power supply is necessary for each artifact, this setup is not used for processing the average artifact.

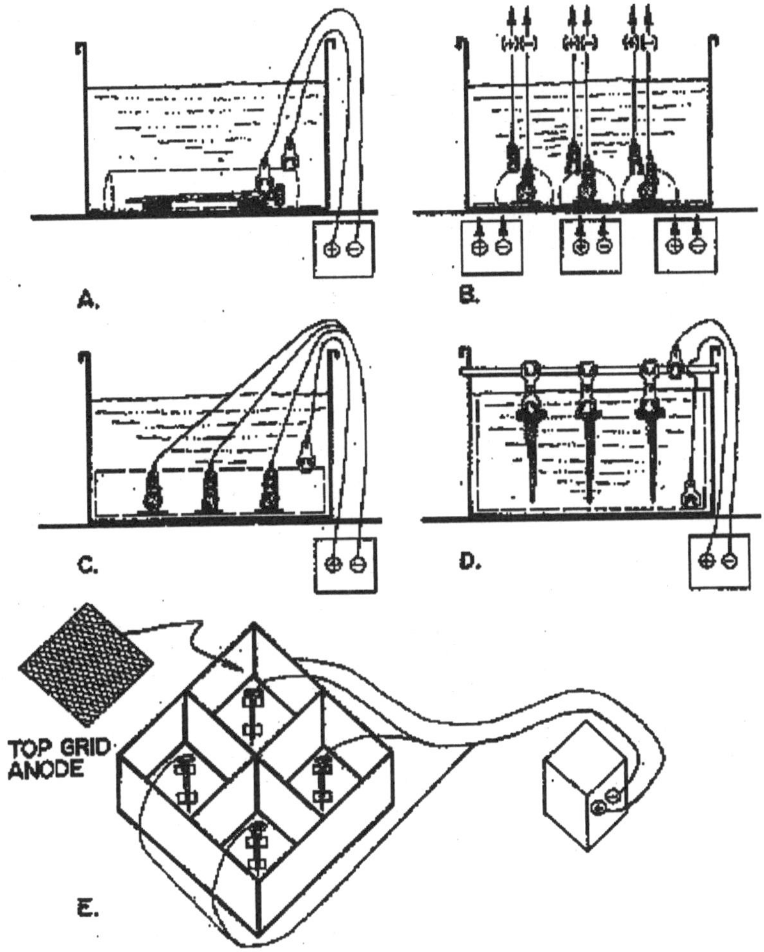

The electrolytic setup may have many artifacts in one container, but each is surrounded by its own close, form-fitted anode, and each one has a separate direct current power supply. When this arrangement is used, it is important to make sure that the distance between the different anodes is greater than the distances between the artifact and its anode in order to prevent any cross-over current. With this setup the current flow to each artifact can be carefully controlled and the correct electrode potential maintained. Since the chlorides present in the electrolyte come from all the artifacts in the artifact. It is drawback that there is not possible to determine exactly when any one is free of chlorides. The chloride test, however, does tell the conservator when to change a chloride-contaminated electrolyte and when all artifact have been cleaned.

If any requires close supervision for consolidate the metal-oxide interface, to preserve some surface or structural detail then artifact should be hooked .There is most critical variable for precision control that is the ability to maintain an even current density on the cathode surface by positioning the anode equidistant from all parts of the artifact while maintaining a steady reduction electrode potential than monitoring of chlorides during electrolysis.

There is number of ways of connecting multiple artifacts to a single power supply and this setup is the most commonly used in electrolytic reduction. Regardless of how it is done, the least desirable from the standpoint of control, but they have the advantage of processing a number of artifacts at one time on one power supply in one container. Each artifact may be individually connected to the negative terminal of a single power supply. The artifacts share common anode sheets placed above and below the artifacts. An alternative variation of this setup has a common bottom anode and individual top form-fitted anodes to assure to even distribution of the current to each artifact.

A setup in which artifacts suspended from a brass cathode rod conductor, with adjustable vertical anode sheets hung to either side, and preferably another anode along the bottom of the container is most popular and known as "sandwich setup". The oxygen evolved off the bottom anode sheet assures that the solution is continually mixed, thus preventing chlorides from concentrating along the bottom of the container. The increased circulation also helps to maintain the anodes in a passive state by preventing strongly oxidizing, acidic hypochlorite from forming at the anode.

This setup has all the disadvantages. In addition to the varied resistance of each artifact, the proximity of the artifact to the negative terminal connection is a factor in the current flow. The closer an artifact is to the negative terminal the more current it receive. If one use this setup, it can be improved by regularly repositioning the artifacts so that for the duration of the treatment, each artifact receives an average current. This alternative has the advantage of making it possible to process a number when of artifacts on one power supply in one container.

(i) Electrolytic Reduction Setups

When a metal container is used as the anode, it should have the adjustable expanded steel anode sheets hung along the sides and at the top to adjust for differences in the size of artifacts. In case plastic container , it is desirable to have a bottom anode because the oxygen evolved from the bottom and should be assures that the solution is continually mixed, thus preventing the tendency for molecular chlorides and hypochlorite to concentrate along the bottom or at the anodes.

It is recommend that three brass rods to be suspended across the top of the container, vertical sheets of steel be hung by copper wire from the side rods, and artifacts can be suspended by copper wire from the center rod (Plenderleith 1956:195) . It is much simpler to use the stainless steel sheets which extend up to the top of the container. It can bent and extended over the ends of the container . This eliminates the two brass anode bars and the copper suspension wires which would in any case go into anodic dissolution and plate the cathode. The anode sheets are attached to the positive terminal with a clip. Since the copper wire attached to the clip is out of the solution it does not go into anodic dissolution and disconnect from the clip, which is a common occurrence on anode connections submerged in the electrolyte.

There should be use the technique of suspending the artifacts by copper wire wrapped around them and the cathode rod is not effective. Inevitably, at some point electrical contact will be lost. So it is more desirable , for most small artifact to attach them with double-ended clips. The clips apply a constant pressure and assure maintenance of a secure contact on the cathode rod and on the artifacts. The clips facilitate attaching and removing to artifacts without unnecessary interruptions and difficulties.

The main disadvantage of this set up is that more difficult to regulate the current to each artifact. Therefore, since the electrode potential or the current density cannot be controlled, the possibility of reducing the appropriate corrosion compounds back to a metallic state is considerably lessened. It is also impossible to monitor the chloride loss from any one artifact.

There can also a number of setups that involve a number of different artifacts, each in its own container, but all can be connected to a single power supply. An artifact can be placed in each of the compartments. When more than one compartment is used, the current to each artifact cannot be controlled, but the chloride level of the electrolyte in each of the compartments can be monitored. This approach takes advantage of limited facilities by using one direct current power supply for several artifacts. It also enables the conservator to determine exactly when each artifact is cleaned of chlorides, thus keeping the length of treatment of any one to a minimum. If treatment of any artifact of any compartment is completed then compartment can be taken down without disturbing the set up and electrolytic treatment in the other compartment.

A single power supply hooked to a control panel consisting of a number of amperage gauges and rheostats is being used by conservators. Each artifact is to be placed in a separate container, and the current to it from the single power supply is to be regulated by means of the rheostat wired in line to it. Each artifact or container has a gage that shows the amperage going to it. This particular setup can be used to regulate the current to a number of artifacts from a single power supply and it has no particular disadvantages if the number of artifacts being treated is kept reasonable. However, conservators have adopted a practice of treating a number of archaeological iron artifacts from a power supply that can only put out 20 amps. The current to each artifact is in the milliamperage. The result is that a lot of artifacts can be put into treatment at a time, but the time to finish a single artifact is dramatically increased. In fact the situation or question arises of whether or not all the chlorides can actually be removed during this exclusively low current density electrolysis. From a multitude of experience, that whatever setup is utilized, that a range of current densities to be used, and at some point in the treatment, it necessary to have a steady evolution of hydrogen from the artifact. Otherwise, this setup should be unsuccessful and a waste of time also.

(ii) Electrolytes used in electrolysis

The only two electrolytes commonly used in conservation for treatment of iron artifacts are alkaline solutions of sodium carbonate and sodium hydroxide. It should be kept in mind that the alkalis and acids used in conservation should be concentrated enough to do the required work, but no stronger. There should be avoid to over cleaning the artifact. The 5% sodium hydroxide solution has been recommended in the electrolytic reduction Plenderleith (1956:194).It is also recommended only a 5% sodium carbonate solution can be used for electrolytic reduction (Plenderleith and Werner (1971:198). No discussion is presented as to the advantages and disadvantages of each electrolyte and under what circumstances one is preferable over the other. In proper conservation procedures, both electrolytes have their uses and the conservator needs to know when to choose the one best suited for the artifacts at hand.

Sodium Carbonate

If maximum reduction is not the objective then 5% sodium carbonate electrolyte with a pH =11.5 will be sufficient for the electrolytic cleaning of most of iron artifacts. Sodium carbonate is much safer to handle and much less caustic than sodium hydroxide. It is less conductive than sodium hydroxide. So it has to be used in stronger concentrations, 5 to 10% versus 2 to 5%. The solubility of sodium carbonate in water is less than sodium hydroxide, which makes it more difficult to mix. Sodium carbonate does not generate the extreme heat when mixed in concentrated solutions but sodium hydroxide generates the extreme heat when mixed in concentrated solutions.

The 5% sodium carbonate electrolyte is to 2% sodium hydroxide electrolyte. An artifact can be treated in 5% sodium carbonate mixed in tap and de-ionized water and 2% sodium hydroxide mixed in tap and de-ionized water. In all cases chlorides seem to diffuse out of the artifacts and reach higher chloride ions concentration in the sodium carbonate electrolyte more quickly than comparable artifacts in sodium hydroxide electrolyte. The major problem encountered with the sodium carbonate is the cathodic precipitates of insoluble carbonate on artifacts. The carbonate precipitates from the electrolyte and is more apt to happen at high current densities and when certain tap water is used to mix the electrolyte.

The carbonate deposit on the artifacts treated in 5% sodium carbonate is much more efficacious or prevalent if the tap water has a large amount of carbonate in it. Artifacts from salt water, encrusted with calcium carbonate, magnesium hydroxide, and other minerals can provide the necessary elements to react with the carbonate in the electrolyte to form insoluble carbonates such as calcium or possibly magnesium carbonate. Once an artifact is plated with a carbonate deposit, it can seal off the surface and chlorides can be trapped inside, misleading the conservator as to when treatment of the artifact has been completed.

When using sodium carbonate as the electrolyte then a white precipitate of insoluble carbonate occurs. The gluconic acid, sodium gluconate or sodium glucoheptanate can be added as a sequestering agent to the electrolyte. There may be decrease in the deposit with the addition of gluconic acid. It will still very apparent on iron artifacts in sodium carbonate in tap water but in the case of slightly noticeable in sodium carbonate in de-ionized water. By adding 2% of the weight of the sodium carbonate in the electrolyte as gluconic acid or sodium gluconate, the tendency to deposit carbonate is reduced but not always eliminated. For maximum effectiveness gluconic acid or sodium gluconate require an excess of a free base ie hydroxide. The pH = 11.5 of 5% sodium carbonate is to be too low for maximum effectiveness. To eliminate the carbonate deposit test with sodium glucoheptanate which acts as a sequestering. If the precipitate is not noticed, then there is no reason to go to the trouble of adding a sequestering to the electrolyte.

When carbonate deposit does precipitate on the iron artifact then it is not required to brush off or remove by electrolysis. The carbonate deposit can, however, be eliminated by soaking several days in a 5% solution of sodium sesquicarbonate or sodium hexametaphosphate. Sodium sesquicarbonate complexes with the insoluble calcium or magnesium salts to form soluble salts in the form of sodium hexametaphosphates (Plenderleith and Werner 1971:250-253).

Some other major problems commonly encountered with a sodium carbonate electrolyte. The pH and conductivity of the solution are not adequate to keep the mild steel anodes passive in the presence of high chloride levels. In the sodium carbonate electrolyte hydroxyl ions discharge as oxygen at the anode more readily than the dissociation products of carbonate ions. The anode becomes acidic due to the accumulation of hydrogen from the oxygen evolution reaction; therefore, anodic dissolution is more prevalent than when sodium hydroxide with its surplus of hydroxyl ions, is used. To avoid this mild steel anode must be cleaned and replaced more often than in sodium hydroxide, especially if the electrolyte is not circulated. It has also been noted that takes longer to rinse out all residue of a sodium carbonate electrolyte than to it does to rinse out all residue of a sodium hydroxide electrolyte.

The most important disadvantage of sodium carbonate relates to its pH and cathode reduction potentials. Theoretically, more efficient reduction of a ferrous corrosion compound is possible using 2% to 5% sodium hydroxide with a pH=12.9 than 5% sodium carbonate with a pH =11.5. In general, sodium carbonate can be used as an electrolyte if reduction is not the objective, but when it comes to treating metals from archaeological site, sodium hydroxide is to be preferred.

Sodium Hydroxide

By using 2 to 5% sodium hydroxide with its higher pH the shortcomings of 5% sodium carbonate are overcome for the electrolysis of iron artifact. However, sodium hydroxide electrolyte being much more caustic, constantly presents a potential. This is hazard to conservators who are working with it. During use of these chemicals, caution has to be taken, and adequate safety equipment such as gloves, eye shields, eye washes, and safety showers should be available at working site. In spite of these problems, a 2% solution of sodium hydroxide is the only option. The objective is to reduce corrosion products. It is the standard electrolyte to which most of conservators treated iron artifacts recovered from the archaeological sites,

Gluconic acid, sodium gluconate, or sodium glucoheptanate in the amount of 2% of the sodium hydroxide or sodium carbonate in the electrolyte can be added as a precautionary measure and a sequestering agent to prevent the precipitation of insoluble calcium carbonates which come from residue of the encrustation and the electrolyte, onto the artifact being electrolytically cleaned is a problem. In addition to preventing undesirable deposits on the cathode, the gluconate ions act as rust inhibitors which keep the steel anodes clean by sequestering dissolved ferric ions which would ordinarily precipitate as ferric hydroxide or oxide. They also prevent the artifacts from rusting during rinsing and drying.

2. Effect of electrolytes on metal container

When iron artifacts from the archaeological site are cleaned in the metal container there may be a very large build-up of chlorides in the electrolyte for the first few baths. There may be high level of chloride about 2,000 to 18,000 ppm , depending upon the artifact recovered from the which environment and lack of external circulation can cause the anode ,the metal container , to corrode extensively through anodic dissolution. The problem can be worse with 5% sodium carbonate . So it should not be used in container that are not easily replaced. Corrosion is still encountered with 2% sodium hydroxide even with its higher pH =12.9. By using a 5% sodium hydroxide electrolyte with its surplus of hydroxyl ions, anodic dissolution is more easily prevented. After the chloride levels drop below 1000 ppm, 2% sodium hydroxide can be safely used.

3. Role of water in electrolyte

In the case of electrolysis of iron artifacts only distilled or de-ionized water is to be employed in preparation of all types of electrolyte. The artifacts are to be cleaned may have heavily contaminated with chloride. Then de-ionized water is a substitute. The use of tap water in the first electrolytic baths may actually reduce the electrolysis time. Chlorides are removed more rapidly when tap water rather than deionized water is used in the sodium carbonate and sodium hydroxide electrolyte.

It has been recommended for cleaning by electrolytic reduction by starting to 2 to 5% sodium hydroxide in tap water for the artifacts recovered from archaeological sites. At low current density the reduction of ferrous compounds is attempted and high levels of chloride are removed. Until the chloride measurements approximate the level found in the tap water reduction is continued in the tap water electrolyte. The tap water can be replaced by deionized water, electrolysis is continued with 5% sodium hydroxide or lowered to 2% sodium hydroxide . Until the electrolyte is again changed a low current density is maintained, thereafter a medium current density is to be used.

When the objective is the reduction and consolidation of ferrous corrosion products the higher pH of sodium hydroxide is preferable.

Sodium hydroxide should be used as the electrolyte. There is no advantage in using sodium hydroxide and sodium carbonate. If corrosion products are in a ferric state . This is applicable to many iron artifacts. That are air-oxidized in archeological sites but this generalization should not be carried out too far. There will almost always be some ferrous compounds that can be successfully reduced.

4. Current Density for electrolysis

In the electrolytic reduction the current density used is expressed as the number of amperes per unit of square area, introduced in the electrolytic cell by external D.C. power supply, such as one ampere per square centimeter (1 amp/cm^2). Any given current density should have a given objective of conservation of iron artifacts. Current densities from 0.001 to 1 amp/cm^2 have been proposed. (Plenderleith 1956:156 Plenderleith and Torraca 1968:342; Plenderleith and Werner 1971 :198; Townsend 1972:252; Pearson 1972:12).

Approximately 10 amps per square decimeter (1 amp/cm^2) of cathode area so as to give a steady, vigorous evolution of hydrogen. This density is not critical for iron and steel artifacts (Plenderleith and Werner1971:198). If the artifact is solid and well-consolidated and has only ferric corrosion compounds then current rate is not critical. If the artifact has ferrous corrosion compounds, an initial high current density will quickly flake off the corrosion layer and significantly alter the shape of the artifact. The initially high current density can disfigure the surface of artifacts and also seal off, preventing the removal of deeply seated chlorides. These type problems can be avoided by using a low current density in the early stages. To consolidate the metal, oxide interface may be through a reduction process and thus preserve a closer approximation of the artifact's actual dimensions. This is also applicable in the case of wrought iron artifacts whose corrosion layers are often non-adherent.

It has been recommonded the following current densities and objectives:

Low current density 0.001-0.005 amp/cm^2 attempts to approximate the reduction range of ferrous corrosion compounds. Moderate current density, 0.05 amp/cm^2 attempts to approximate the optimum conditions for chloride removal without undue evolution of hydrogen. High current density of 0.1amp/cm^2 has as its major goal the vigorous evolution of hydrogen for mechanical cleaning.

The above current densities are recommended for treating to the iron artifacts from the marine archaeological sites. These current densities are established by measuring the electrode potential established first on the surface of a rectangular bar of steel and then verified on a number of small artifacts. The artifact should be started off at a low current density for iron reduction as objective. For the long time chloride removal stage a medium current density is to be followed. The continuation of low current density would only lengthen the process, while the vigorous production and evolution of hydrogen at high current density interferes with the efficient removal of chloride from the metal and its corrosion products. The encrustation at the low current density and medium current density are slowly removed corrosion products and scale from the artifacts by the mechanical action of the evolved hydrogen. There should be finished the chloride from artifact at a high current density for maximum efficiency. This insures the complete removal of any remaining encrustation and loose corrosion layers or scale, as well as any remaining chlorides. When high current density in electrolysis is used in the last state of electrolysis the metal corrosion products that is capable of being reduced and have been reduced and it is less likely that they will be removed by the vigorous evolution hydrogen. While the above densities serve as useful guidelines, they cannot be adhered to rigidly. Thus, in the case of very large artifacts, these calculations might require current in excess of the maximum capacity of a power supply.

Due to irregular shapes and size ,it is difficult to determine the square area of many iron artifacts to use the current densities. The calculated area should be concerned only with the cathode area that is exposed opposite an anode. The total area of the cathode is used only when an anode is form-fitted around all sides of the cathode; otherwise, only that area exposed to an anode is used. Any given current density determines the electrode potential established between the electrodes and the electrolyte and the rate of hydrogen evolution at the cathode. For the reduction of metallic corrosion compounds, the establishment of a certain electrode potential on the cathode is essential. Since there is not a one-to-one relationship between a given current density and a corresponding electrode potential on differentially corroded iron artifacts and different iron alloys. The current density alone is not the ultimate guide. The calculated current densities are simply not a fine enough tool for precision treatment.

To start the electrolysis at an applied voltage of 1.8 volts D.C. and to continue treating the artifact at this voltage for at least one week (North 1987:226). To the evolve hydrogen above voltage is usually not sufficient, but it does reduce the highly reactive materials present in the artifact and sets up the artifact so that a hydrogen potential graph can be developed for that particular artifact. In the end of the first week of electrolysis the point, as indicated by voltage, is found where the current, as indicated by amperage starts to increase rapidly. The chart is made starting with points much lower than the point of hydrogen evolution and increasing the voltage well above the point of hydrogen evolution. By graphing the intersection points, with amperage as the x-axis and volts as the y-axis, it is easy to see where the voltage that corresponds to the point at which the amperage starts to increase rapidly. This is the hydrogen evolution voltage. The electrolysis is then conducted at this voltage. By using this technique, some of the difficulties of using current densities are eliminated.

To measurement of current densities and establishment of hydrogen evolution voltage is necessary for most of the artifacts. Start the electrolysis off by slowly increasing the voltage until first began to observe the evolving of few bubbles of hydrogen. For metal reduction do not need any hydrogen evolution at all in the theory point of view but the irregular evolution of hydrogen from the surface of the metal gives one a visual indicator that the current is flowing. It is the evolution of first evidence of hydrogen evolution that the voltage is not the indicator in this technique. However, after a short time, the evolution of hydrogen increases as the resistance of the artifact is broken down and there is some reduction of the corrosion products in the metal. So decrease to setting back to the point where hydrogen first starts to evolve. After going through this low hydrogen evolution, where the objective is to reduce as much of the corrosion products as possible, the current is increase so that there is a steady, not vigorous, evolution of hydrogen. This is necessary if one wants to remove the maximum amount of chlorides within a reasonable length of time. Maintaining a very low current density , current will only prolong the process an unacceptably long time and not contribute any other benefit. One may choose to run the artifact for a few hours or days at a high current density that is for maximum mechanical cleaning as per option (North 1987:226).It is depend on:

1. Visual evolution of slow, irregular evolution of hydrogen for maximum reduction.
2. Visual evidence of a steady evolution, not vigorous, of hydrogen for the much longer process of chloride removal.
3. A vigorous evolution of hydrogen for final mechanical cleaning to remove any last remaining encrustation or loose corrosion products.

By treating, a series of carefully measured artifacts at different voltage and measuring the resultant electrode potential is how can derived the current densities. Over a period of time, and electrode potential measurement validated it, that is necessary and visual indicator of the rate of hydrogen evolution through treatment. In the case of iron, most of the corrosion products, if they can be reduced, are reduced to magnetite. It has not been shown that any of the corrosion products actually reduce back to metal, as in the non-ferrous metals. By considering electrode potential, it also clearly shows why one electrolyte is preferred over another, when maximum reduction is the objective.

5. Electrode Potentials for electrolysis

The normal electrode potential, or relative activity, of each metal is based on an electromotive series on the hydrogen scale.

Metal		Reaction
4. Gold (+1 aurous, +3 auric)	↑	$Au^{+3} + 3e^{-} \longleftarrow\!\longrightarrow Au + 150$
3. Silver (+1)		$Ag^{+} + e^{-} \longleftarrow\!\longrightarrow Ag +.799$
2. Copper (+1 cuprous)	(+)	$Cu^{+} + e^{-} \longleftarrow\!\longrightarrow Cu+0.552$
1. Copper (+2 cupric)		$Cu^{+2} + 2e^{-} \longleftarrow\!\longrightarrow Cu+0.337$
0 Hydrogen (+1) +0.0	□	$\mathbf{2H^{+} + 2e^{-} \longleftarrow\!\longrightarrow H_2}$
1. Lead (+2 plumbus, +4 plumbic)		$Pb^{+2} +2e^{-} \longleftarrow\!\longrightarrow Pb - 0.126$
3. Tin (+2 stannous, +4 stannic)	(-)	$Sn^{+2} + 2e^{-} \longleftarrow\!\longrightarrow Sn - 0.136$
4. Iron (+2 ferrous)		$Fe^{+2}+2e^{-} \longleftarrow\!\longrightarrow Fe-.440-0.409$
5. Iron (+3 ferric)		$Fe^{+3} + 3e^{-} \longleftarrow\!\longrightarrow Fe - 0.036$
6. Zinc (+2)	↓	$Zn^{+2} + 2e^{-} \longleftarrow\!\longrightarrow Zn - 0.763$

The normal electrode potential of each metal is in comparison to a normal hydrogen electrode. Since there is no practical means of measuring a single electrode potential without reference to another single electrode potential. The hydrogen electrode is given an arbitrary potential of zero and all metals are negative or positive to it. The normal electrode potential of a metal represents the EMF. This required balancing the cell formed by a particular metal electrode immersed in a solution of its salt of normal cation activity and a hydrogen electrode (Evans 1963:231).

The potential series of the metals represent their equilibrium values at a pH = 0. These potentials change with pH value. In order for a metal to be corroded anodically, a potential more positive than the equilibrium value must be established and for the cathodic reduction, a more negative potential must be created. Cathodic reduction of iron becomes pronounced only if the potential is made considerably more negative than the equilibrium value. Dissolution of the anode becomes significant when the potential is made considerably more positive.

The potentials of the metals are altered if the ionic activity or effective concentration is not normal. If the solution is diluted, the passage from the ionic to the metallic state will be slower, whereas the passage from the metal into solution remains unaltered. Thus the balance will be upset, but a fresh balance may be obtained at a more negative potential. This means that at 18° C, if activity and concentration are as identical, every ten-fold dilution, from N to N/10, or from N/10 to N/100 will shift the potential in a negative direction by 0.058 volt for a monovalent ion, or 0.029 volt for a divalent ion. The theoretically, the shift of potential is approximately realized in the case of the more noble metals. But for the less noble iron metal the potential actually measured is found to be almost independent of the concentration of the metallic salt in the original solution. When the metal is capable of reacting with the solution then this type of activities occurs. So that the concentration in the layer next to the metal becomes different from that in the body of the liquid (Evans 1963:234).

The potential of iron immersed in an aqueous solution originally free from iron ions depends on the hydrogen-ion concentration, becoming steadily more negative as the pH value rises (Evans 1963:235).

From the electromotive series shows that the reduction reaction of ferrous ions, $Fe^{+2} \rightarrow Fe^{\circ} - 2e$, occurs at - 0.409 -0.440 volts at pH = 0. The reduction potential increases -0.029 volts for each pH increase. The reduction of ferric ions, $Fe^{+3} \rightarrow Fe^{o}$-3e, occurs at -0.036 and increases -0.19 volts per pH increase. The hydrogen discharge potential $2H^{+} \rightarrow H_2$ - 2e occurs at a voltage potential of 0 and increases -0.58 volts per unit pH increase. The reduction potential of ferrous, ferric and hydrogen ions at different pH's and standard temperature of 20° C can be graphically presented as Reduction Potentials of Ferric, Ferrous, and Hydrogen ions at Different pH's and Standard Temperature of 20° C. The pH Range of a 5% Na_2CO_3 and a 2% NaOH Electrolyte are shaded in Fig. 1.

By utilizing the following graph it is possible to determine the theoretical electrode potential voltage necessary for reduction of iron oxides for any given pH.

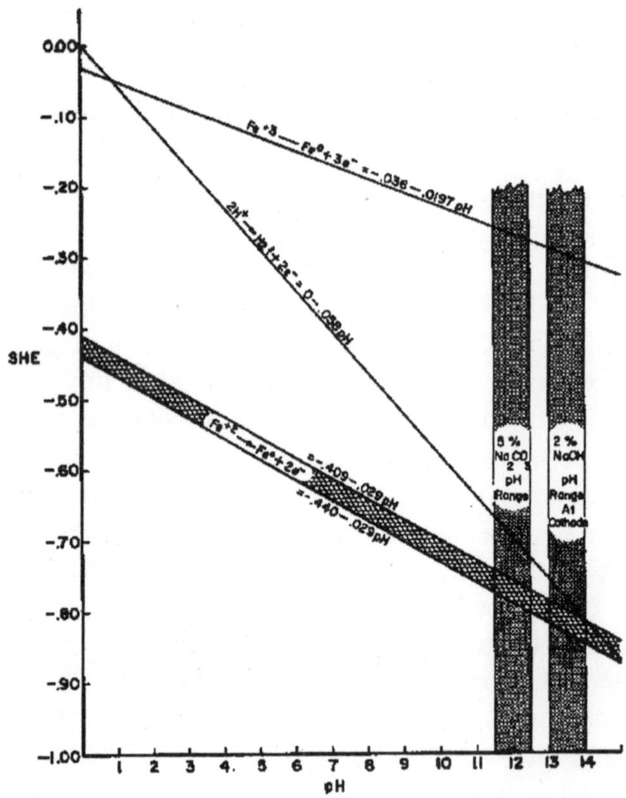

Fig. 1

The cathode electrode potential is critical in the electrolytic cleaning of iron artifact because the hydrogen discharge potential is reached, hydrogen ions are formed, which are utilized to reduce adjacent ferrous compounds. At more negative potentials so rapidly molecular hydrogen is formed and evolves as hydrogen gas by combining the molecules with each other. In this case oxide compounds of iron do not reduce by hydrogen evolved as a gas. But it acts as a mechanical cleaning agent that physically removes any unconsolidated corrosion layers. The theoretical point of view the electrolytic reduction of ferrous ion corrosion compounds is at the intersection of the hydrogen discharge line and the ferrous ion reduction line shown in the figure 1.

By using the formula $Fe^{+2} + 2e \rightarrow Fe^{\circ}$ and substituting values for the Fe^{+2} reduction potential and the correction for pH (-0.409 -0.029 pH) the intersection appears at a pH =14.1 and an electrode potential of -0.82. This potential is reached just prior to the evolution of hydrogen. In dilute aqueous caustic soda, it is possible to establish a maximum pH =14 on the cathode surface. At low current density electrolysis, minimum or no hydrogen is evident; however, the objective is to establish the electrode potential of the intersection of the discharge potential of hydrogen and the reduction potential of ferrous ions or immediately to the left of this intersection on the surface of cathode. The maximum reduction and consolidation of the ferrous corrosion compounds on the theoretically.

Thermodynamically, ferric oxide and other ferric iron corrosion compounds in an aqueous solution are not reduced. The graph shows the reduction electrode potential is out of the range for electrolytic reduction in an aqueous alkaline electrolyte and an external EMF. An electrochemical reaction occurs on a metallic surface in contact with an electrolyte of known pH and ion content by measuring electrode potentials. The electrolytic reduction of metal artifacts is controlled the electrode potential (Hamilton 1976:103-105).

By using electrode potentials there may be determine the current density in an electrolyte of known pH for required establishing the condition most conducive to the reduction of ferrous compounds on the metal.

Once an electrode potential has been established on the surface of the cathode, periodic measurements and adjustments have to be made in the direct current to maintain that potential. After electrolysis has begun, several hours to a full day are required for the cathode to adjust to an equilibrium state. At the metal surface a metal-hydrogen (M-H) bond is established .The surface of the metal becomes saturated with hydrogen and evolution of hydrogen takes place. Until the metal surface becomes saturated with hydrogen the potential shifts. Once equilibrium is established the potentials even out. After establishing an electrode potential on an artifact, daily adjustment may be necessary to maintain the potential as the IR of the electrolyte drops with the addition of dissolved salts and the resistance of the metal and its corrosion products are altered. Before adjusting back to the predetermined potential, one has to be sure that any shift is due to changes in the cathode, and not due to the transport system, i.e. the electrolyte through lack of circulation. The transport system is still adequate, especially at the reduction potentials of ferrous compounds. If any changes occur in the transport system it will become visually apparent at the anode. An alkaline electrolyte is used, acidic areas can form at the anode. In these areas chloride ions react with the positively charged anode to form hypochlorite ions (ClO^-) or hypochlorous acid (HClO) which oxidizes the anode. Adverse reactions are easily detected at the anode, and when this occurs, the cathode is also affected, although it is not as apparent or as detrimental to the operation of the electrolytic cell. The potential at both electrodes is altered, however, a change in the potential occur, the electrolyte should be stirred or circulated and the measurements taken again. If the electrode potential remains the same, then the amperage may be adjusted back to re-establish the optimum range.

From the standpoint of efficiency, electrode potential measurements are necessary for precise control and quality processing of much selected artifacts. The areas of advanced or retarded corrosion will be reflected in the electrode potentials, making it possible for the conservator to identify those areas requiring more extensive reduction and a way to measure the progress of the electrolyte reduction. The data acquired from electrode potential measurements was used to arrive at realistic current densities that established the approximate electrode potentials for the bulk of the iron artifacts that will require treatment but do not warrant the close supervision or the time required for taking potential measurements. Still, there is the difficulty of arriving at current densities for given artifacts, especially irregular shaped artifacts and differentially corroded artifacts. For these reasons, except for those special artifacts, using either hydrogen evolution potential voltage or merely visually observing the rate of hydrogen evolution is sufficient.

2. Outdoor Electrolysis for Iron Artifacts

Any electrochemical reduction cleaning process results in irritating caustic vapors and hydrogen gas, which have to be properly exhausted from any room or building for the safety and comfort of person. For the electrochemical reduction cleaning process following are required;

1. Fume hoods
2. Sealed rooms with exhaust systems
3. The electrolytic container can be placed outside

Above methods can be utilizes by most of the conservators. The smaller artifacts are cleaned under the fume hoods. In a separate room of building few large artifacts can be cleaned which has ventilation facilities. Any air-blown dirt and sand present have no problems. The rain problem can be determined easily with a hydrometer to test the specific gravity, and remedied by adding more sodium hydroxide or sodium carbonate. Rain will only decrease the amount of de-ionized water that needs to be added to the container daily to compensate for evaporation, caustic vapors and electrolytic reduction.

If the area is fairly isolated which should safe from human traffic and has adequate utilities. Then it may be strongly recommended for outdoor electrolytic reduction and could be considered. The sheds over the container are optional and power supplies must be kept out of the weather. Although winter temperatures do not decrease the chemical activity, there can be an IR drop in the electrolyte that will increase the cell voltage.

i. General observation during electrolytically cleaning of iron artifacts

The above observations are directed primarily toward large iron artifacts. Improving the procedure and reducing the time in electrolysis has been recommended. Conservators often avoid cleaning large iron artifacts electrolytically due to their size insurmountable problems. It is better to understand the success or failure of electrolytic cleaning, several case histories are to be reviewed.

Lieutenant Nielsen of Norway was make attempt to electrolytically cleaning to a large wrought iron artifact with inadequate facilities (Eriksen and Thegel 1966:100-102). The attempt was unsuccessful for a number of reasons:

1. Failure to remove the wooden under carriage shielded a large portion of the artifact
2. Prevention of an even distribution of the current.
3. Treatment was too brief to remove the chlorides.
4. It lasted a total of 69 discontinuous hours spread over a 384-hour period.
5. The placement of the steel anode sheet along only one side of the container failed to assure an even distribution of current.
6. The wooden undercarriage was swabbed with hydrochloric acid to neutralize the 1% sodium hydroxide used as the electrolyte after the brief electrolytic treatment.
7. This acid introduced additional chlorides to attack the iron.

Ora Patoharju (1964, 1973) reports one of the first successful attempts to clean a large cast-iron artifact which was sunk. The artifact served as the cathode with three stainless steel sheet anodes in a 10% sodium carbonate electrolyte. They are run at a rate of 20 amperes at 4 volts (current density 027 amps/cm^2) for one month and a rate of 150 amperes at 4 volts (current density 2 amps/cm^2) for five months.

The preliminary conclusion of Patoharju is that wet cast-iron artifact coming directly from the ocean can be conserved by electrolysis in a liquid phase. If the artifact is allowed to dry out before treatment the artifacts may undergo further oxidation and any conservation attempt may be futile. Leaving of the maximum corrosion layer when intact on the artifacts. After completion of the treatment it may be decided to put them back into treatment in order to darken the surfaces. Melted wax applied on the artifact. Artifacts probably caused increased conversions of FeO to

Fe_2O_3 and they may put back into electrolysis. The corrosion layer completely detached, leaving a badly disfigured surface in the both cases. The treatment must be successful on the first time if thick layers of corrosion are present. The nature of the wrought iron corrosion layers are non-adherent and after the water is removed from the corrosion layers during the drying and sealant steps, they apparently undergo additional oxidation and may also lose the electrical couple with the metal core. Hydrogen will evolve at the surface of the metal and slough off the corrosion layer during subsequent electrolysis. Perhaps this can be alleviated by soaking the artifact in electrolyte for a long time to re-establish the electrical couple prior to any further electrolysis.

ii. Exposure to anode surface

Single mild steel can be used as anode along one side of the container and used immovable electric resists support cradles on the artifacts. The placement of the anode failed to assume an even current density and the cradles shielded two areas from what current flow is present. Minor corrosion may be occurred at these two support points because the artifacts may not rotated sufficiently during the treatment. At the similar occurrences at support points and even on small surface areas covered with plastic identification tape. Any portion of the artifact should not be covered throughout electrolysis, for even a small piece of narrow tape can shield the area beneath sufficiently to prevent complete removal of the corrosive chlorides. To avoid this, artifacts should be rotated frequently and the position of movable supports, such as bricks, should be shifted each time the electrolyte is changed. When numbered plastic tape is placed on artifacts for purposes of identification, the position of the tape should be moved at least once during electrolysis.

In the case of the importance of form-fitted anodes when electrolytically, cleaning artifacts the conservation literature has failed to emphasize to it. An anode placed to assure an even current density over all the surface of the artifact and improves the efficiency of the process. Now by form-fitted, it is not mean that there is an exact distance maintained between the artifact and the anode. This is nearly irregular shaped artifacts. It means for artifact, especially irregular shaped artifacts, bend and shape the anode so that is some what evenly distanced form the anode (North 1987:225) .The use of form-fitted anodes that have been shown to be unnecessary as long as the artifact-anode distance is between 20-80 cm a satisfactory current distribution will be achieved. However, a rod is used as the anode of an artifacts, this does not apply, for the current will be concentrated in the bore because of the small distance between the rod and the artifacts. While discussing on the establishment of hydrogen evolution potential voltage. It is stated that if the hydrogen gas evolution is coming from only one area of the artifact, that there is either a poor electrical contact at this point or that the anode is too close to the artifact at that point (North 1987:226). Obviously, an anode shaped to çonform to the shape of the artifact is recommended even if no one does not do it in everyday conservation, usually placing artifacts between two anodes. In any case, a form-fitted anode, will maximize iron reduction and chloride removal, and will cut down on the electrolytic time. Since all areas of the artifacts should be exposed to anode surface, immovable supports, lifting frames, and such things as wooden undercarriages on artifact should be avoided.

iii. Duration of Electrolysis

The aspect of the preservation of artifacts is the short electrolysis time, six to eight weeks, and the long rinse period, up to five months. The full potential of electrolysis is not to be achieved. If time has permitted a longer electrolysis period, it is probable that the rinsing time could have been substantially cut.

Ora Patoharju (1964) reported an electrolysis time of six months to clean iron artifacts recovered from an archaeological site. Every wrought iron artifact approaching the more size has required between six and twelve months of electrolysis. As an example of the length of time required for large wrought iron artifacts. It is reported that an artifacts 6'7" long, required around 20 days to remove all the encrustation and to dismantle the component parts, 251 days of electrolytic cleaning at 20 to 50 amps, one weak of rinsing in several changes of alternate boiling and cold deionized water and two weak dehydrating in alcohol, and one and a half days submerged in molten microcrystalline wax. For example if three hopped barrel cannons processed together in one container required 480 days of electrolysis, three months of rinsing, about one weak of dehydration in alcohol, and one weak submerged in microcrystalline wax. Even small wrought iron artifacts such as spikes often require 60 to 90 days of electrolysis.

iv. Reducing Electrolysis Time

When artifacts are electrolytically cleaned in small container with a low volume of electrolyte to artifact volume, the length of electrolytic time is considerably extended. To cleaning the artifact for shorter the period by electrolysis the larger volume of electrolyte is required. Two wrought iron that may clean in two small containers required around two years of electrolysis. It follows that more frequent changes of the electrolyte will considerably speed up the process also.

Several aspects of shortening the length of electrolytic treatment have been worked out. The problem of reducing the chloride ions level in the electrolyte below 50 to 100 ppm so chloride ions requires the greatest amount of electrolytic time. Below 100 ppm chloride ions the artifact is presumably in the final stages of cleaning. There are at least two explanations for this long electrolytic time:

The electrolysis is carried out at high current densities, which have a tendency to repress chloride ions migration in preference for H_2 evolution. The chloride ions concentration in the electrolysis is governed by the Donnan equilibrium equation.

The Donnan theory pertains to the unequal distribution of ions on two sides of a membrane (Kunin 1958:14-16). Although no membrane exists between the artifact and the electrolyte, the interface between the solid and liquid phases may be considered as a membrane. An exchange of chloride ions continues until the concentration ratios are equal in both phases. The lower the chloride ions ratio in the electrolyte, the more effective the diffusion of the chloride ions from the artifact to the electrolyte. Using the Donnan equilibrium theory, it can be generalized that the rate of chloride ions transfer from the artifact to the electrolyte is negated despite the electrolytic field when the chloride ions content of the electrolyte is higher or equal to the chloride ions level in the artifact. This results, according to the Donnan theory, because Chlorine one = Chlorine two , i.e., the chloride ion concentration of two solutions in contact will equalize. As a result, chloride tests can be mislead under equilibrium conditions. Negligible or no increase in the chloride reading in the electrolyte over several days may lead the conservator to believe that the chloride removal has been accomplished and terminate electrolysis, leaving deep-seated chlorides in the artifact.

For optimum efficiency in electrolysis, the chloride level of the electrolyte should be less than the chloride level of the artifact. When the chloride ions content in the electrolyte maintains a steady level in a controlled constant volume of electrolyte, it is apparent that:

Equilibrium conditions have been obtained and unless the electrolyte is renewed to lower the chloride ions concentration, little or no chloride ions removal from the artifact .

The chloride removal process can be completed.

- By changing the electrolyte this can be easily validated.
- By frequently changing the electrolyte and using as large a container as possible, principles of the Donnan equilibrium equation can be used to the conservator's advantage.
- The lower the chloride ions level in the electrolyte, the greater the driving force for chloride ions removal, which translates as Time and Efficiency.

Decreases in required electrolytic time could be achieved with other artifacts treated in larger volumes of electrolyte and when the electrolyte is changed . It is crucial to the electrolytic process for a satisfactory quantitative chloride-monitoring test. The chloride tests allow the conservator to determine the rate and efficiency of the chloride removal.

d. Chemical Cleaning

A number of chemical cleaning procedures are used for iron artifacts from non-marine environments when negligible chlorides are present. The most common chemicals are oxalic acid, citric acid, phosphoric acid, ethylenediamine tetra-acetic acid (EDTA), and other complexing agents. Because of the problems of chlorides in iron from the ocean and archaeological sites, the exclusive use of any of these may improve the appearance of an artifact, but they do not remove chlorides and hence cannot prevent subsequent corrosion. Therefore, they are not considered as conservation alternatives for treating iron from salt water (Plenderleith and Werner 1971).

Two chemicals, phosphoric acid, along with its derivatives in commercial rust removers, and tannin solutions, are often used to form a corrosion-resistant film of phosphate and tannates on the surface of treated iron artifacts . The corrosion-resistant significance of phosphate and tannate films is to be first made apparent and also gives an excellent state of preservation even in the case of oldest iron artifacts (Farrer, Beck and Wormwell 1953). Before either chemical can be used, however, the chlorides must be removed by electrolytic reduction, alkaline sulphite, or water diffusion.

i. Tannic Acid

Tannic acid is a plant product organic compound , specially extracted from the myroblans family. Knowles and White (1958) and later by Pelikan 1966 were investigated tannate films as a corrosion-resistant for iron artefacts. It was found in accelerated exposure tests that tannate films on iron were more corrosion-resistant and lasted twice as long as a phosphate-coating. Solutions of hydrolysable tannins such as chestnut, myroblans, or valonea extracts with a pH = 2 to 2.5 provide the most weather-resistant protection (Knowles and White 1958). Phosphoric acid should be added to bring down to a pH = 2.4. If the tannic acid mixture has high a pH. It is important that the right tannic acid should be selected as many are not effective. Tannic acid solutions ($C_{76}H_{52}O_{46}$), with a pH = 2.5-3.0 provide good weather-resistant tannate films. Tannic acid solutions are a standard part of the conservation of all iron artifacts. Although some conservator use the tannic acid as the final step. The microcrystalline wax may be use as coating, which is applied over the oxidized tannate film for maximum protection.

The several coats of 20% tannin solution (200 g. tannin, 1 liter water and 150 ml. ethanol) is applied with a stiff brush for the maximum protection. A film of brush provides better protection in comparison to a dipped or sprayed application because the brushing assures that the solution has access to the metal in areas of loose rust and eliminates the polarization of cathodic areas by the formation of hydrogen (Pelikan 1966112). The cast iron artifacts may be successfully treated by vacuum-impregnating with a tannin solution. The artifact is allowed to completely air-oxidize between each application of the tannic acid and left to dry one to two days after the final application.

The tannin solution reacts with the iron or iron oxide to form a ferrous tannate with oxidizes to a mechanically strong, compact blue-black colour ferric tannate. It should be to assure to form a continuous film of ferric of tannate. Knowles and White (1958) recommend that all the iron oxide be removed, otherwise, they contend, there is a possibility that corrosion may start at the junctures of the cathodic iron oxide and the tannate film. Tannin solutions react directly with the metal base and with the rust if the solution is acidic, pH=2 to 3. The tannin solutions can be used to impart an aesthetically pleasing black colour to iron and forming a corrosion-resistant film.

A 20% solution of phosphoric acid (H_3PO_4) applied on iron artifacts by impregnating and there form a phosphate film. This film is formed with impregnation the solution under a vacuum and should be assuring to complete penetration into all the porous areas of the metal. An inert film of ferric phosphate is form on the surface of the metal by the action of said acid complexes with the iron. Rees-Jones (1972) reported that porous cast iron artifacts were successfully treated by this method after removing the chlorides by water diffusion. Similar results are achieved on wrought iron or steel.

A mixture of phosphoric acid and tannin solution can be used on badly rusted iron and it appreciably improves the corrosion resistance of a phosphate film (Pelikan 1966:112-113). One hundred milliliters of 80-85% phosphoric acid solution is added to the 20% tannin solution and several coats are brushed on the artifact, then at least four coats of the standard 20% tannin solution is brushed on the artifact. The treatment to an iron artifact with the mixed solution of phosphoric acid or tannin, a final sealant should be applied to seal off the tannate or phosphate film. It may noted that phosphoric acid and tannic acid solution does not form the dense black colouration.

Logan (1989) recommends mixing up 1 liter of a 10% tannic acid solution of tannic acid (100 g. tannic acid, 50 ml ethanol, 900 ml deionized water) and if necessary, add sufficient concentrated phosphoric acid so that the solution has a pH = 2.4. A 10% solution of tannic acid is much too concentrated and recommends that several coats of diluted 2-3% tannic acid be brushed on the artifact. In this case does not recommend using a sealant over the tannic acid, but instead recommends controlled storage.

Only the 20% mixture of tannic acid can be use to treatment to marine iron and this give consistently good result. Never attempted to use a 2-3% solution of tannic acid on marine iron. A sealant, such as microcrystalline wax can be applied over the ferric tannate film. The wax will provide a vapor barrier, which the ferric tannate film does not, and will also contribute some strength to corrosion layers on the metal.

e. Annealing

i. Oxidizing Atmosphere

The iron artifacts can be treated by heating at a temperature of 850°C (Eriksen and Thegel 1966). The chemically bound water associated with the ferrous chloride corrosion products in the porous matrix of the metal would be driven off at this temperature and leaving inactive anhydrous ferrous chloride. The leaving chlorides in an anhydrous state will not prevent subsequent corrosion. Both ferrous and ferric chloride are deliquescent, capable of absorbing water from the atmosphere and reinitiating the corrosion process unless a perfect airtight, atmosphere-proof coating is applied. The success of annealing in the air is probably due to the sublimation of the chlorides. Pearson (1972:25) conducted experiments and indicate that a temperature of 850°C is well above the melting point of ferrous chloride, and both ferrous and ferric chloride sublimed strongly iron artifact at 700° C. The sublimation of ferric and ferrous chlorides occurs at a temperature of 700°C and higher temperature.

When elevated the temperatures alter the metallurgical micro-structure of the metal, making it useless for future metallurgical examinations. Due to these shortcomings, the technique of annealing in an oxidizing atmosphere is not recommended.

ii. Reducing Hydrogen Atmosphere

Barkman and Franzen 1972, has demonstrated that annealing iron at a temperature of 1060°C and in a reducing atmosphere successfully stabilizes and preserves it, returns it to a metallic state, and eliminates by sublimation the corrosive chloride compounds.

The iron artifacts to be heated in the presence of hydrogen gas and treated in a hydrogen gas furnace . The temperature is slowly elevated to 1060°C. over a period of one week. All the moisture is driven off and all the chloride corrosion compounds are volatilized at this elevated temperature. The iron corrosion compounds reduced in back metallic state by hydrogen and hydrogen combines with the oxygen in the corrosion products from water, which is driven off by the heat. In a reducing atmosphere annealing damage very little to the surface of the metal. Extensive experiments and research are needed in this case, however, to determine the extent of any undesirable surface alteration.

The lack of hydrogen kilns sizeable to treat large artifacts and the expense of the equipment even for small artifacts is the primary drawbacks to the technique. When the chlorides are driven off the large amount of hydrochloric acid produces and which attack any exposed metal in the kilns or furnaces. It is a drawback of this treatment technique.

Artifacts in size of about 10 inches by 4 feet can be usually treated by this technique. Artifacts can be preserved by this process and in most instances they remain stable, even though in most cases they can be annealed in an oxidizing furnace and the surface are badly oxidizing. There is some controversy over possible side effects the heating and cooling have on the surface of corrosion layers and the morphology of the metal.

Over the years the temperature to which the hydrogen oven is taken has been decreased. The artifacts undergoing hydrogen reduction can be placed in a special furnace with 100% dry hydrogen gas, or a mixture of hydrogen and nitrogen and heated to a temperature of 300°C and over a period of days taken to 1000° C (Barkman 1978:155-166).All the moisture is driven out of the artifact and the chloride corrosion compounds are volatilized during the treatment. The iron corrosion compounds reduced by the hydrogen in a lower oxidation state or metal. Hydrogen also combines with oxygen in the corrosion products, forming water which is driven off by the heat. This treatment has several drawbacks. First it requires rather expensive and sophisticated equipment. Second, there is the problem of the changes in the metallurgical characteristics in the metal when heated to high temperatures (Tylecote and Black 1980:95) .

The loss of information by the treatment of totally rusted cast iron artifacts at 800°C will not be great and there seems to be little objection to the use of the hydrogen reduction process at 800 °C for this purpose. The reduction of rust on wrought iron is a different matter. The main problem knows whether the residual metal contains enough carbon to give useful information to the archaeometallurgist. If Carbon is absent in the artifacts then treatment at 380°C is acceptable although some change will occur. The slag inclusions will suffer very little microscopic change. But there is no microscopic change in slag. It may be ensure to the removal of chlorides at 380 °C the treatment time must exceed 60 hours.

The conservator can follows the process of treatment annealing in a reducing atmosphere of hydrogen. The main limiting factor is the inherent safety concerns and potential danger of heating hydrogen to these temperatures. The treatment given result in stable, chloride free artifacts.

iii. Hydrogen Plasma Reduction

Hydrogen plasma reduction is a latest and new technique (Patscheider and Vep_ek 1986). In this technique, iron artifacts, as well as those of copper and silver, can be conserved by placing them in a quartz discharge tube surrounded by hydrogen gas under a low pressure which is ionized into plasma by the introduction of high frequency radio waves. The process involve for conservation is iron in the center of the hydrogen plasma and the magnetite and ferric oxide on the piece are converted to metallic iron. This treatment is carried out at a temperature of less than 400° C and there is no change in the metallic structure of the iron.

The primary disadvantage of this conservation technique is the high cost of the equipment and the small size of the artifacts that can be treated at all but the most expensive units. A unit capable of treating a single artifact in a chamber about 30 cm x 10 cm. Thus far, the technique has not seen out use in most conservation laboratories.

iv. Water Diffusion

There will always be some artifacts that can not be conserved or any the treatments given during archaeological excavation. Any electrochemical or chemical treatment would considerably alter the form of the artifact . There may not be little or no metal remain on the artifacts. Then three main choices are possible. The chlorides can be removed by a process referred to as water diffusion, the artifact can be embedded in plastic.

The only way an iron artifact recovered from the sea can be stabilized is to remove the chlorides from the artifact . This is most easily accomplished by electrolytic reduction techniques, but if the artifact is very badly oxidized, and the overall form and dimensions of the artifact are to remain intact, the only alternative is to remove the soluble chlorides in the much slower process of water diffusion (Oddy and Hughes 1970). In this process, the artifact is placed into a container filled with water, and the water is changed frequently as the soluble chlorides diffuse out of the metal into the solution. The water should be changed by determination a qualitative or quantitative test of chloride. However, water diffusion is not an option for all intent and purpose. By this process the total chloride removal is not possible within any accepted time frame when any other option is available. When attempting to conserve badly corroded artifact there may be chances of destroyed if cleaned by electrolytic reduction or by the alkaline sulphite treatment.

Since water diffusion requires a long time so that water must be inhibited to prevent the metal from rusting. Alkaline chemicals, such as a 5% sodium sesquicarbonate, 5% sodium carbonate, or 2% sodium hydroxide solution, serve only as inhibitors to prevent rusting. Only water is removing the soluble chlorides from the artifact by this process. For removal of chloride from chloride-contaminated iron, the solution is made with tap water until the maximum chloride level approximates that of the tap water; then deionized water is substituted. Uninhibited deionized water should not be used in water diffusion because it is very corrosive.

Organ (1955) suggested the alternating hot and cold temperatures, which speed up chloride removal by alternately expanding and contracting the capillaries in the metal and the corrosion layer, causing a flushing action of expelling and drawing in fresh water. From a standpoint of coefficients of thermal expansion, however, the alternate heating and cooling probably changes the diffusion gradient of the solution rather than significantly changing the size of the metal capillaries. This will decrease the time required to remove the soluble chlorides in some instances. Oddy and Hughes (1970) found that there was no significant difference between the times required to wash similar artifacts at room temperature. The alternated heating and cooling cycle may facilitate the treatment, however, when significant levels of chloride are present and months to years are required to remove them. After the complete elimination of soluble chlorides, the artifacts need to be carried through the same final steps as iron treated by other methods.

3. Final Conservation Steps

a. Rinse after Treatment

One of the following conservation treatments can be selected by the conservator for the treatment of iron artifacts - electrochemical, electrolytic, chemical, or water diffusion. The removal of insoluble oxide sludge, metallic powder, residual chlorides and all the chemical residues through an intensive rinsing is necessary (Plenderleith and Werner 1971). In the water diffusion and electrolytic reduction or the artifact is removed after establishing that the chloride count in the solution has leveled off and ceases to rise when it is changed. The artifact is then removed and rinsed thoroughly in several changes of alternate boiling and cold de-ionized water to get rid of any residual electrolyte and chlorides. The surface of the metal oxidizes to a flat black color that provides a pleasing appearance by rinsing in boiling water. Large artifacts may require two to four weeks of rinsing, the iron may rust in the de-ionized water. The rust can be prevented by adding gluconic acid, sodium gluconate or sodium glucoheptanate. The gluconates act as rust inhibitors during any washing and continue to serve in this capacity during solvent dehydration, heat-drying or air drying. Iron artifacts can be prevented from rusting during the rinse process by washing with a potassium chromate solution (1000 ppm chromate) with a pH not lower than 8.5. But the strict disposal requirement of chromate solutions. Neither the gluconates nor chromate solutions are used widely nor are satisfactory results achieved.

The artifact is allowed to stand in the last conatainer of rinse water for a minimum of 24 hours. A sample of the bath water is taken and acidified with nitric acid and tested with 0.2 N silver nitrate for the presence of chloride. The silver nitrate test is suggested because it is quick, qualitative, and quite sensitive to minuscule amounts of chlorides. If the test is positive the artifact is returned either to electrolysis or further rinsing. If the test is negative the artifact is ready to be dried and sealed with microcrystalline wax.

The iron artifacts treated by water diffusion are put through a similar rinsing process. Since, however, many of the artifacts treated by water diffusion can be in very fragile condition, they may not be able to stand the mechanical action of boiling water. The rinse water, if heated, is kept below the boiling point. Sodium glucoheptanate could be added to the rinse water as a rust inhibitor.

b. Qualitative Test for Chlorides

We can determine the presence or absence of chlorides by the silver nitrate test (Plenderleith and Werner 1971). For the chloride test we placed the artifact in distilled or de-ionized water for a few hours or overnight. A 10 to 20 milliliter sample of the water solution is placed in a test tube and acidified with a few drops of dilute nitric acid (10%). The solution is mixed and five drops of 0.2 N silver nitrate (17 grams of $AgNO_3$ /1 liter of H_2O) is added. The test tube is held against a black background with good side lighting. If any chlorides are present a white opalescence will be apparent. Under ideal conditions, with clean glassware and uncontaminated reagents, the test provides a good qualitative indicator for the presence or absence of chloride. We may do confirmatory test also for the confirmation of the other interfering agents during the chloride test.

c. Drying

Before applying any sealant on the artefacts, the moisture absorbed by the artifact must be removed after rinsing, except certain waxes which are heated above the boiling point of water, can be applied. When artifact depend upon the physical and chemical condition can be immersed in any wax heated above the boiling point of water then drying is an optional step. Artifact drying can be accomplished by heat, vacuum desiccation, or dehydration in water-miscible alcohol or acetone. The metal surfaces are in a reactive state and quickly rust on exposure to air after treating iron. By applying tannic acid to the surface the contact with air should be minimized. If the black coloration is desired, or the final sealant or insulating coating is applied to the artifact in order to prevent superficial rust that quickly forms on the surface. Some exposure to air is inevitable and it is particularly troublesome when drying by heat (ovens or infra-red lamps) or vacuum desiccation. To prevent rust formation on the surface gluconate rinses could be helpful. The infra-red lamps are not very effective on dense artifacts.

As an alternative method a water-miscible solvent, ethanol, methanol, isopropanol, or acetone is to be use for rinses the iron artifacts after treatment. Isopropanol is more suitable because it is nontoxic, has a higher flash point and does not have an obnoxious odor. Ethanol and acetone are even more effective but have some disadvantages also. Each of these solvents surmounts the problems of rusting when exposed to air and can be used on artifacts of any size. For the artifacts with little core metal remaining drying in an oxygen-free environment is preferable. Such as environment provided by alcohols is necessary to prevent the remaining metal from rusting and ferrous compounds from oxidizing to a ferric state. The artifacts is to be expand and slough off the oxide layers by above both reactions .The role of alcohols are also have the advantage of enhancing the removal of any remaining soluble chlorides and water in the artifacts. When the artifacts are still in the alcohol all stains and undesirable features can be removed by brushing. Artifacts can be stored in alcohol until it have convenient to conservation process. Artifact is removed while the water is hot and wiped with rags after completion of the water-rinsing. This allows most of the water to evaporate before giving it a preliminary rinse in alcohol that has been previously used for drying wet artifacts to remove the bulk of the remaining surface water. There after submerged in the water free isopropanol to dehydrate for a minimum of 24 hours. By taking these precautions the water content of the alcohol bath is kept low and it can be used for long periods. When the water content becomes sufficiently high it is used for the preliminary rinse and fresh alcohol is used for the dehydration bath. This efficiency procedure is very important.

d. Sealant and Consolidation

The first step in preventing material of corrosion understands its specific mechanism. The second and often more difficult step are designing a type of prevention. Some metals produce corrosion products that are insoluble, about the same size molecular as the parent metal, and that crystallize in the same type of lattice structure. These are often able to become attached to the metal surface and form a protective coat against further corrosion.

Other preventive measures involve the use of protective coatings and modification of the environment. Some trace impurities can significantly reduces the rate of corrosion and can be added in low concentration to the surrounding medium. Paint is the most common coating used to slow the rate of atmospheric corrosion. Many other materials, such as plastics, ceramics, rubbers and even electroplated metals can be used as protective coatings but these materials are prohibited in the case of iron artifacts since the esthetic value of these artifacts are affected.

After treatment of sea-recovered iron artifacts it is imperative that their surfaces be covered with a protective coating to insulate the metal from the effects of moisture, chemically active vapors, and gases. It is highly important to choose the right sealant or coating to provide a protective moisture barrier and prevent corrosion. In general, the sealant selected should be:

Impervious to water vapors and gases, natural-looking so that it does not having the tendency to lessen from the appearance of the artifact, reversible, and transparent or translucent so any corrosion of the metal surface can be quickly detected.

Various monomers, acrylates, acetates, epoxies, paints, oils, lacquers, and other sealants have been used in the past, but few have to resist the test of time. Many craze, peel are irreversible, or have a high degree of permeability to water vapour. No one sealant is completely successful and all have some disadvantages, but microcrystalline waxes best satisfy the requirements of conservation. Most importantly, they are the least permeable to water vapor of any of the sealants commonly used (Rudniewski and Tworek 1963:212). They have a high melting point and are relatively hard waxes. Besides sealing the surface of the artifact from the atmosphere and moisture, they provide considerable stability and strength to artifacts and are excellent for consolidating fragile artifacts. Microcrystalline wax is highly recommended in both cast iron and wrought iron that is to be stored and displayed indoors. In contrast, some laboratories use microcrystalline wax as the final coat only on cast iron artifacts (North 1987 : 207-252).

Cosmoloid 80H is the most often-recommended microcrystalline wax seen in much of the conservation literature. The Gulf 75 Micro-wax and Witco 180M microcrystalline wax are also effective. Both melt at approximately 80°C and have been satisfactory, although Gulf 75 is a little harder and more brittle.

In some instances it may be advisable to dewater, dry or dehydrated the artifact in alcohol before it is placed in a container of microcrystalline wax; however, when microcrystalline wax is used as the final sealant it is possible to eliminate the drying process for many iron artifacts. The wax is heated at 176° C , well above the boiling point of water. Therefore, it is possible to take the artifact directly out of the water rinse and place it in melted wax. As the temperature of the wax rises, any water in the artifact is vaporized. The artifact must be kept in the wax long enough and at a high enough temperature to completely vaporize the water. Since the water boils out of the artifact, this alternative should not be used on fragile artifacts or artifacts with a loose oxide layer. These fragile artifacts should be dried by one of the methods mentioned above. With this exception, combining the water removal and the sealant steps remain a very satisfactory approach. Time and expense are saved and good results are achieved.

If the artifact is in fragile condition, all the alcohol must be evaporated; otherwise, the vaporization of the alcohol in the corrosion layers by the hot wax can damage the artifact. The artifact is left in the wax until all bubbles stop evolving from the artifact. This may require several days for large artifact. After complete penetration the wax is cooled from 93° C to 107°C, the artifact is removed and the excess wax is promptly wiped off with rags.

The temperature at which the artifact is removed determines the thickness of the wax coating. Too low a temperature results in an obvious layer of wax, while at too high a temperature all the wax runs off. After cooling, if any excess wax should remain, it can be removed with a proper equipments. The last-named is the simplest method and leaves the least obvious scars on the wax film. Additional wax or wax with graphite added to it as a pigment can be used to cover the surface defects in the metal and enhance the appearance of badly corroded artifacts.

To impregnate in large artifacts with microcrystalline wax if facilities are not available, so various other coatings must be used like chromate paints, lacquers, clear epoxies, linseed oil, and polyurethane. In general polyurethane are found to be ineffective. Over a period of months they crazed, peeled, and became permeable to moisture. The opaque coatings hid the surface of the artifact from view, preventing one from observing the corrosion occurring under the coating. In addition, the surface finish of the epoxy is too glossy and irreversible, causing further damage to a few artifact which may require re-treatment.

Polyurethane based paints or coatings are thermoplastic polymers that have many favorable attributes for serving as a protective coating on treated iron artifacts. They form clear, fast-drying, hard, flexible coatings with excellent adhesion that are highly resistant to moisture, salt water, acids, alkalis, abrasion, impact, and weathering. The coatings can be removed with aromatic and chlorinated solvents such as toluene or ethylene dichloride. Polyurethane comes in gloss and stain finishes. The gloss finish has more resin and is therefore more durable. It is recommended for outdoor use. The satin finish has less resin and has silica added to give a more acceptable flat finish, but it is less durable than the gloss finish and is generally recommended for indoor uses. By using an undercoat of gloss and a second coat of satin finish and by adding graphite to one or both coats, a very acceptable, translucent finish can be obtained that does not detract from the underlying surface colour of the specimen being coated.

The iron artifacts can be coated with a 20% tannin solution to form a corrosion-resistant ferric tannate film on the surface of the artifacts. The applied surface may allow to air oxidize for two days, changing the gray surface colour of the artifacts to a more pleasing blue-black colour. The artifacts then can be painted with a coat of clear gloss polyurethane, allowed to dry and then painted with a coat of satin polyurethane. Graphite may be added to both the gloss and the satin polyurethane to completely dull any glossiness to the surface finish. The results will be very satisfactory. The use of polyurethane coatings in the manner described above or by them can be recommended for maximum protection of large iron artifacts to be displayed outside or in areas of high humidity and salt vapor in the air (Hamilton 1976:55; North and Pearson 1975:177; North 1987:230-231).

The wrought iron artifacts to be displayed indoors, after drying with commercial dewatering fluids , using clear drying zinc phosphate-based anti-corrosion primer as the first coat, followed by up to 6 sprays of high durability, clear, acrylic lacquer, and finished off with a final coat of krylon mat spray finish (North and Pearson 1975:177, North 1987:230-231).

With the exception of microcrystalline wax, which is easily removed by placing the artifact in a container of boiling water, all the others present some problems. For ease of application, resistance to water vapor, the presence of chloride, transparency, ability to strengthen the surface of the artifact, microcrystalline wax stands out for use on both cast iron and wrought iron that are stored and displayed indoors. If any artifact displayed outdoors it should not be treated with microcrystalline wax . Since it accumulates dust on the its surface. Instead of microcrystalline wax polyurethane based paints is recommended for the artifact which are to be display out side.

The large artifacts to be displayed outdoors by using a coating made up to three parts zinc silicate powder mixed with two parts water (Townsend 1972: 253). This mixture forms a light beige paint that oxidizes to a light nautical gray. The coating, being anodic, provides cathodic protection of the iron artifact and is said to be highly resistant to salt spray, rain, sunshine, and temperature fluctuations. Large artifacts can be painted with zinc silicate and displayed outdoors.

Artifacts that are so badly corroded they cannot be treated, and compound artifacts with metal and organic parts requiring treatment but which cannot be separated, can be embedded in clear plastic blocks. Selectron -5000 resins can be used for embedded wrought iron (Smith and Ellis 1961:32-35). This technique is drastic, with no hope of ever extracting the artifacts from the blocks, but it remains a possibility for every selected problematic artifact.

e. De-watering

The surface layers of metals after cleaning will behave in the same way as a mass of capillary tubes, retaining water. So removal of water and complete drying of the metal surface is necessary to prevent further corrosion after coating. Drying or removal of the entrapped pore water can be done by:

a. Placing the artifact in a dry area and using hot air blowers to speed up the evaporation process and
b. Using chemical dewatering agents.

The advantage of chemical dewatering agent is that it can also be used as a carrier for incorporating a corrosion inhibitor into the graphitized surface.

f. Preservative Coatings

After removal of chloride ions, the corrosion products layer in cast iron consists of finely divided graphite (cathodic), iron (anodic) and iron corrosion products (mainly FeO) with 30-60% by volume water in the pore spaces. This composition, being very unstable, will corrode in presence of air and moisture from the atmosphere if left unprotected. The graphitized surface may also be soft and prone to physical damages.
The metal surface in marine wrought iron, after cleaning, is both physically and chemically stable. The surface is made up of bare and very rough metallic iron with iron oxides and slag in crevices. Water can accumulate in these crevices and cause renewed corrosion if not protected

properly. Surface coatings are much simple and effective for wrought iron than cast iron. As marine iron contains water in the pores and capillaries, so before surface coating it must be dried thoroughly.

A. Tannin Coating Method

1. Cast Iron

Small cast iron artifacts are removed from the final wash solution, then washed in a flowing de-ionized water, wiped dry and finally allowed to drain for 15-20 minutes. The artifacts are then submerged completely in acetone for about 1 hour, after which they are brought out and allowed to drain and dry in the air. This may take about 10-20 minutes. The artifacts are transferred to a solution of 3% W/V of tannic acid in methylated spirit and kept completely dipped into the solution for around 1 hour after which they are removed and allowed to dry again . Tannic acid is deposited in the graphitized zone, thus protecting the artifact as it acts as a corrosion inhibitor. It is considered important to dry quickly in hot air at 260°C (Organ R.M 1978:22). Crystals of tannic acid crusting the surface is brushed off with a soft brush. It can also be used to adjust the black surface if considered desirable. For large cast iron artifacts immersion in acetone and tannic acid solution is desirable, but is difficult and very expensive. So here dewatering agents are brushed liberally into the artifact surface over a period of 2-3 hours. An industrial hot air blower can be used to accelerate drying after application of acetone or methanol. Alternative commercial dewatering agents, with lower flammability and which usually contain some type of iron corrosion inhibitor can be used.

2. Wrought Iron

Wrought iron does not have many problems as cast iron as they have a metal surface with only a thin layer of oxides. They are dewatered by brushing a commercial dewatering agent, liberally on the surface and allowed to dry.

B. Coating by Waxes

As microcrystalline wax is the best coating material for iron artifacts, so after drying, the iron artifacts are generally coated with it. The wax used for coating to the cast iron should have a melting point between 70-90°C, adhere well to the iron surface, be slightly pale in colour and biologically inert. It must be hard enough to resist deformation under steady pressure but not so hard as to become brittle when struck or tapped.

1. Cast Iron

The small amount of wax is enough for covering the small cast iron artifacts. It should be taken in a suitable container and heated in oven at 110-130 °C. Then melted wax is applied . The artifact is wrapped in wide-wire mesh with sufficient surplus mesh protruding above the top of the wax when artifact is immersed into the wax bath.

The artifact is dipped into the wax bath until bubbling stops. This takes between 1-2 hours after- which the artifact is left in the wax for another 2 hours to ensure that impregnation is complete before allowing the wax bath to cool down. During cooling, when the first sign of solidification occurs the artifact is removed from the bath and left to cool on a heat resistant surface, which would not form strong bond with the wax. The complete cooling and solidification of the wax-impregnated artifact may take around 24 hours. After cooling excess wax is removed by a knife or scalpel and the surface cleaned with white spirit or gently brushed with soft bristle brush. The artifact must be stored or displayed in dry and dust free environment.

Shellac can be used on upper surface give a sealant coat which can be easily cleaned to remove dust (North N.A 1988:207-254). Shellac paint is prepared by dissolving shellac powder in methylated spirit in the ratio of 1g :2 ml. It gives a shiny black finish on the surface. For large cast iron artifacts wax impregnation involves a high cost. So a solution of wax in a hydrocarbon solvent is applied by brush. When the solvent slowly evaporates, a coating of wax is left on the artifact surface. 6-10 coats of the wax must be applied over a few days so as to build up a substantial wax coating. Here the penetration of wax is not good, generally attaining only 5-10 mm of the outermost layer of graphitized zone. During coating of the graphitized zone occurs as in molten wax impregnation where any moisture of solvent left in the graphitized zone before immersion is evaporated out by the high temperature involved. So complete moisture removal from the artifacts is very important before applying the wax solution. Cast iron artifacts must be stored and displayed indoors in a dry environment and where they are safe from vandalism and accidental damage.

2. Wrought Iron

The commercially available paints for modern iron can be used. As the metal surface can still have some chloride residues, so the paint used must have high chloride tolerance. It must give adequate protection on very rough surfaces and can be removed if necessary.

At western Australia museum, for indoor display two coats of a clear phosphate-based primer ,Kephos 253 ,a Dulux paints, are being used followed by upto six spray coats of high durability clear acrylic lacquer, Dulux-No,298/1055 , diluted with three parts Duco thinner (North N.A 1988 : 207-254).

To get a matt appearance, a coat of matt spray, Kruylon matt's spray finish No.1311, is to be applied. This paint system is found to preserve the natural colour of the wrought iron. Infact the paint is virtually invisible. Chloride tolerance is up to 80-100 ppm on iron surface without any failure.

The disadvantage is that the paint degrades relatively rapidly in high UV light levels and is unsuitable for outdoor display. For outdoor display a fish oil based paint, Rustolium, which comes in a variety of colours but not clear, can be used. Its life span is around 10 years. Sodium hydroxide is used to remove this paint.

For longer life, more than 15 years, a polyurethane based paint (Imperite 390) can be used. Paint is removed by sandblasting. Permanent outdoor displays for wrought iron artifacts must be discouraged as neither of the paints systems mentioned above are perfect. Chlorinated rubber industrial paint pigmented with red-iron oxide was found to be satisfactory for at least 4-5 years for coating iron (Organ R.M 1978). Incralac was found to be very difficult to remove from electrolyzed wrought iron after five years with steel wire brush or even commercial paint removers. (Organ R.M 1978).

g. Storage and Periodic Inspection of Iron Artifact

The preservation of antiquities should produce artifacts that are chemically stable with an aesthetically acceptable appearance. Treatment should be reversible in the event the artifact should require additional preservation; after an artifact has been completely processed it can deteriorate. Only if stored or displayed under optimum conditions this can be prevented. Atmospheric pollutants, Sulphur dioxide, hydrogen sulphide, sodium chloride, dust, and soot are detrimental, ubiquitous, and difficult to control even inside a reasonably tight building. Even more critical is the relative humidity in which an artifact is stored. The moisture level at which corrosion appreciably accelerates is called the critical humidity and is considered to be 60% for iron and steel (Cornet 1970:443). If iron still contains chlorides (theoretically it remains doubtful that all can be removed), a humidity as low as 50% may have to be maintained. Below this critical humidity, subsequent corrosion sometime in the future is inevitable. All the potential corrosive factors should be taken into consideration when storage facilities are being planned.

Since metal artifacts can eventually become chemically unstable from a myriad of causes and may need additional treatment, periodic inspection, and evaluations of the artifacts are necessary. A conserved artifact of iron from a marine site, remains a piece of metal, just as susceptible, and in fact more susceptible, to continued corrosion as any other piece of iron. Proper conservation does not assure one of artifact preserved in perpetuity. At our present stage of knowledge, perhaps it is most realistic to say that the objective of antiquities or iron artifacts conservation is to delay by proper storage reprocessing as long as possible and to make any necessary treatment simple and brief. There remains a lot of room for improvements in the conservation of iron. Still, at our present state, there are a number of procedures that successfully contend with the majority of problems encountered when conserving iron.

BIBLIOGRAPHY

1. Agrawal D.P. 1984; The Archaeology of India. pp 19,137-151and203-210.
2. Agrawal O.P., Hari Narain,Jaiprakash1991; *Historical Metallurgy*. Vol 24(2) pp-81
3. Agrawal O.P.,Hari Narain, Jaiprakash 1991 ; *Historical Metallurgy*. Vol 24(1),pp 12-26
4. A.K. Biswas 1984; Principle of blast furnace in iron making . pp 6-13,53-68,189
5. Argo, James 1981 ; On the Nature of Ferrous Corrosion Products on Marine Iron. *Studies in Conservation* .Vol.26 pp 42-44.
6. B. Bandyopadhyaya ;Survey of Indian Metal Sculpture. pp 51-61
7. Barker B.D. Kedell K. and O Shea DC 1980; The hydrogen reduction process for the conservation of ferrous objects conservation of iron .Editors: Clarke, R.W. and Blackshaw, S.M. pp 23 –27
8. Barkman, L. 1975; Corrosion and Conservation of Iron. In Conservation in Archaeology and the Applied Arts. pp 169-171. IIC , London
9. Barkman, L. 1975. Corrosion and Conservation of Iron. In *Conservation in Archaeology and the Applied Arts*. pp 169-171. IIC, London.
10. Bhardwaj, H.C., 1979, *Aspect of Ancient Indian Technology*.
11. Cornet, J. 1970; Corrosion in Archaeology. In *Scientific Methods in Medieval Archaeology*, edited by R. Berger, pp. 437-454. University of California Press, Berkeley.
12. Craddock P.T., 1995; Early Metal Mining and Production, pp. 156-202, 234-275.
13. Craddock P.T., 2009; Short Term Course on Archaeomaterials.
14. Florian M.L.E 1988 ;The underwater environment conservation if marine archaeological objects. Butterworths series in conservation. pp 1- 20.
15. Fenn, J. D. and K. Foley 1975; Passivation of Iron. *Conservation in Archaeology and the Applied Arts*. Pp 195-198. IIC, London.
16. Frazier F. 1974 ; Production of Artifact Casts Using Epoxy Resin. *The American Archeologist* . Vol 1 pp 33-42.

17. Gellings P.J. 1985; Introduction to Corrosion Prevention and Control.
18. George A, Roberts andRobert A. 1980; Cary Tools Steels. pp 304-307
19. Gilberg, M. R., and N. J. Seeley 1981; The Identity of Compounds Containing chloride ions in Marine Iron Corrosion Products: A Critical Review. *Studies in Conservation* Vol.26 pp 50-56.
20. Gilberg, M. R., and N. J. Seeley 1982; The alkaline sulphite reduction process for archaeological iron .a closer look. *Studies in Conservation* .Vol27 pp 180-184.
21. Hamilton, D. L. 1973; Electrolytic Cleaning of Metal Articles Recovered from the Sea. In *Science Diving International*, edited by N.C. Flemming, pp. 96-104. Proceedings of the 3rd Scientific Symposium of CMAS, 8-9th October 1973. British Sub Aqua Club, London
22. Hunsberger, J. F. 1974; Electrochemical Series. In *Handbook of Chemistry and Physics*, 55th edition, edited by R. C. Weast, pp. D120-125. CRC Press, Cleveland, Ohio.
23. Jain K.C. 1977; Pre-history and Proto-history of India . pp 158-264
24. Keen S. Orton C 1985 ; Stabilities of treated archaeological Iron; an assessment . *Studies in Conservation* .Vol 30 pp 1 36-139
25. Khatibul-Huda ; Protective coatings in conservation of metallic antiquity conservation of metals in Humid climate ICCROM/ NRLC. pp 88-100
26. Kranz, M. 1969. Inhibitors and Stimulants of Corrosion. *Conservation of Metal Antiquities*. Translated by J. Dlutek, pp 17-30. The Scientific Publications Foreign Cooperation Center of the Central Institute for Scientific, Technical, and Economical Information, Warsaw, Poland.
27. Kuppuram G 1989; Ancient Indian Mining Metallurgy and Metal Industries .pp-25-136
28. Knowles E., and T. White 1958 ; The Protection of Metals with Tannins. Journal of Oil and Colour 41:10-23.
29. Leigh D. 1973; Reasons for Preservation and Methods of Conservation. Marine Archaeology, edited by D. J. Blackman, pp. 203-218. Butterworths Publication, London.
30. Logan, J. 1989; Tannic Acid Treatment. Canadian Conservation Institute *Notes* 9.5. Canadian Conservation Institute, Ottowa
31. Mickey C. D. 1980; Artifacts and the Electromotive Series. Journal of Chemical Education 57(4):275-280.
32. Muncher, D. A.1988; Composite Casting of Partially Degraded Iron Artifacts. *Studies in Conservation* 33 pp94-96.
33. Mahmud Syed Jafery 9881; Metal Technology in Medieval India. pp-16-24,60-103

34. North N. A. 1987; Conservation of Metals. *Conservation of Marine Archaeological Objects*, edited by C. Pearson. pp 207-252. Butterworths, London.

35. North, N. A. and I. D. MacLeod. 1987; Corrosion of Metals. *Conservation of Marine Archaeological Objects*, edited by C. Pearson, pp. 68-98. Butterworths Publication , London.

36. North, N. A. and C. Pearson. 1975a; Investigation into Methods for Conserving Iron Relics Recovered from the Sea. *Conservation in Archaeology and the Applied Arts*, pp.173-182. IIC, London

37. North N.A 1988; Conservation of metals conservation of marine archaeological objects . Butterworth's. pp 207 - 254.

38. North N.A. and Pearson C 1978; Washing methods for chloride removal from marine iron artifacts. *Studies in conservation.* Vol. 23,pp 174-186,

39. North Owens and Pearson 1976; Thermal stability of cast and wrought marine iron. *Studies on conservation* . Vol. 21. pp 192 - 197.

40. North N.A. and Pearson C 1977; Thermal decomposition of FeOCl marine cast iron corrosion process, *Studies in Conservation*. pp 146 - 157.

41. North N.A. 1982; Corrosion products on marine iron . *Studies in conservation* . Vol. 27, pp 75-83.

42. North N. A. 1976; Thermal Stability of Cast and Wrought Marine Iron. *Studies in Conservation.* Vol 21 pp75-83.

43. Oddy W.A. and Hughes M.J 1970 ; Stabilization of active bronze and iron antiquities by use of sodium sesquicarbonate. *Studies in Conservation* .Vol 15 pp 183 – 189

44. Organ R.M 1978; Conservation of iron objects found in salty environments. Editor ORGAN, R.M.

45. Patoharju O. 1964; Corrosion Problems in Marine Archaeology. In *Current Corrosion Research in Scandinavia*, edited by J. Larinkari, pp316-323. Kemian Keskuliitto, Helsinki

46. Pearson, C., 1987a; *Conservation of Marine Archaeological Objects*. Butterworths, London.

47. Pearson C.1972; preservation of Iron Cannon after two hundred years under the sea. *Studies in Conservation.* Vol 21 pp192

48. Pelikan, J. B. 1966. Conservation of Iron with Tannin. *Studies in Conservation* Vol.11(3) pp 109-115.

49. Peterson, C. 1974. The Nature of Data from Underwater Archeological Sites. *Underwater Archeology in the National Park Service*, edited by D. Lenihan, pp 62-65. National Park Service, Department of Interior, Washington DC.

50. Patscheider J., and S. Veprek. ; 1986. Application of Low-Pressure Hydrogen plasma to the Conservation of Ancient Iron Artifacts. *Studies in Conservation.* Vol.31 pp 29-37.
51. Plenderleith H. J., and A. E. A. Werner. 1977. *The Conservation of Antiquities and Works of Art.* Oxford University Press.
52. Pearson C 1988; Storage and conservation of marine archaeological objects Butter worths Publication . pp 105 -116.
53. Plenderleith H. J., and Torraca G. 1968. The Conservation of Metals in the Tropics. *The Conservation of Cultural Property. Museum and Monuments.* Vol.11 pp 237-249. UNESCO, Paris
54. Potter, E. C. 1956. Electrochemistry: Principles and Applications. Cleaver-Hume, London
55. Rees-Jones S. G. 1972. Some Aspects of the Conservation of Iron Objects from the Sea. *Studies in Conservation.* Vol 17(1) pp39-43.
56. Pourbaix M. 1966. *Atlas of Electrochemical Equilibrium.* Pergamon Press, Brussels.
57. Robinson, W.S. 1982. The Conservation and Preservation of Ancient Metals from Marine Sites. *International Journal of Nautical Archaeology* .Vol.11(3) pp221-231
58. Roy T.N. 1983; The Ganges Civilization , pp1-20and165-181
59. Rogers Howard. T 1968; Marine corrosion . Newness International Monographs of Corrosion Science and Technology. pp 1-46, 117 – 137and 272,- 281.
60. Ram Dhamija ; Art and Craft in India, pp 1928-1988
61. Rozenfeld I. L1972; Atmospheric corrosion of metals ; An official NACE publication. English Language, Edition (1970), Nace, Houston, Texas . pp. 121-123.
62. Rheodore A. Wertime and James D Muhly 1980; The Coming of the age of iron. pp69-90
63. R.John Sedriks 1979, Corrosion of stainless steel .
64. Robinson W.S. 1981; First aid for marine finds Handbooks in marine Archaeology No.2 National Maritime Museum Greenwich
65. Scott D. A., and N. J. Seeley. 1987. The Washing of Fragile Iron Artifacts. *Studies in Conservation.* Vol 32 pp73-76.
66. Swcheitzer Philip. A 1997 ; What every engineer should know about corrosion. Editor: william H. Middendrof, Marcel Dekker, Inc. New York and Basel. pp 5 -22.
67. Smith, J. B., Jr., and J. P. Ellis. 1961. The Preservation of Underwater Archeological Specimens in Plastic. *Curator* .Vol6(1) pp. 32-36.
68. Susan L. Huntington ; The Art of Ancient India. pp 532-538.

69. Selwyn L.S., W.R. McKinnon, and V. Argyropoulos ; Models for chloride ion diffusion in archaeological iron. *Studies in Conservation* .Vol.46(2) pp109-120.
70. Tylecote R. F., and J. W. B. Black. 1980; The Effect of Hydrogen Reduction on the Properties of Ferrous Materials. *Studies in Conservation* .Vol.25 pp87-96.
71. Tylecote R.F 1976; A History of Metallurgy. pp11, 25,59-63
72. T. Stembolov ; The Corrosion and Conservation of Metallic Antiquities and Works of Art. PP-68-115
73. Turgoos,S 1985. The Corrosion of Archaeological Iron During Burial and Treatment. *Studies in Conservation.* Vol.30 pp13-18.
74. Turgoose S 1980; The nature of surviving iron objects, conservation of iron, Editor Clarke, R.W. and Blackshaw S.M. pp1-7
75. Turgoose S 1982; Post excavation changes in iron antiquities .*Studies in Conservation* . Vol. 27 pp 97-101
76. Townsend S. P. 1964. The Conservation of Artifacts from Salt Water. *Diving into the Past*, edited by J. D. Holmquist and A. H. Wheeler, pp 61-64,. Minnesota Historical Society, St. Paul.
77. Townsend 1972 ; Standard Conservation Procedures. UNESCO. Under Water archaeology. pp 251-256.
78. Ulick R. Evans 1979; The Corrosion and Oxidation of Metals.
79. Von Fraun Hofer J.A. 1974; Concise Corrosion Science, published by Portculli s press Ltd. England. pp. 1 -46,117-137, 272 –281.
80. Werner A. E. A. 1968. The Conservation of Metals in the Tropics. *The Conservation of Cultural Property. Museum and Monuments* .Vol.11 pp 237-249. UNESCO, Paris.
81. Western A. C. 1972. The Conservation of Excavated Iron Objects. *Studies in Conservation* .Vol. 17(2) pp 34-40
82. Walker R.; 1982. The Corrosion and Preservation of Iron Antiquities. *The Journal of Chemical Education.* Vol. 59(11) pp 943-947.
83. Watkinson D 1980; An assessment of lithium Hydroxide and sodium Hydroxide treatments, for archaeological ironwork. Conservation of iron . Editors Clarks, R.W. and Blackshow S.M. pp 28 – 40.
84. Watkinson, D. 1983. Degree of Mineralization: Its Significance for the Stability and Ttreatment of Excavated Ironwork. *Studies in Conservation,* Vol.28 pp. 85-90.
85. Wihr, R. 1975. Electrolytic Desalination of Archaeological Iron. In *Conservation in Archaeology and the Applied Arts*. pp189-191. IIC, London.
86. Yu.M.Lakhtin 1977; Engineering Physical Metallurgy and heat treatment . pp 140-143.

INDEX

F

G

H

I

V

W

Z